# RISE & REACH
## Life and Leadership

# RISE & REACH
## Life and Leadership

§

*Written by*
*Dana Rondel*

Partners
In
Goodwill
*publications & media*

*What Inspiration Sounds and Looks Like.*
www.partnersingoodwill.com

This book is a work of non-fiction. People, places, events and experiences are the product of the author's experience. Any resemblance to other persons, living or dead, or historical events, is purely coincidental.

ISBN: 978-0-9817291-7-6
ISBN: 0-9817291-7-7

Dana Rondel, Founder and Lead Minister of *Wisdom In New Dimensions (WIND)* and Founder of *Partners In Goodwill* Publications & Media, speaks before small and large audiences. She shares her gifts of inspiration and wisdom with all who love to be informed, inspired and uplifted. Visit Dana Rondel's web sites to discover more, and to book her for a speaking engagement:

www.danarondel.com

For more about *Wisdom In New Dimensions* (WIND), visit:

www.windinc.org

For products, services and other books by Dana Rondel and that are available through *Partners In Goodwill*, visit:

www.partnersingoodwill.com

*This book is dedicated to **Life** —*
*for without Life, we could not*
*experience The Gifts of **Mind**…*

Love, blessings and gratitude:
*Divine Inspiration*

...we
*rise and reach*
greater and loftier heights...

— Dana Rondel

## Higher Truth One

Many believe in the Omnipresence of God
(Spirit, Divine Love, Infinite Intelligence, Universal Creative Force, Allah, Jah, Jesus Christ,
Yahweh, Brahman etc.), nonetheless, it seems
difficult for individuals to believe in the
ubiquity of Good...If God is everywhere, at all
times, then it must be the same for Good
(God). In spite of appearances, circumstances,
and present experiences, there is nowhere in
life or in the world where there isn't Good.

- Dana Rondel

## Higher Truth Statements

*Higher Truth Two*

Our daily work is to prosper our lives mentally, emotionally (heartfully) and physically — holistically, so that we become fully connected with our Greatest and Highest Selves (Our God Soul), which then allow us to more completely realize our relationship with The Most High. It is our relationship with The Most High that opens up within us a deeper and stronger awareness of our truest potential as a Spiritual People — Full Beings... We, as Full Beings, then know without fear, doubt or worry that we can do all things through God who strengthens Us...

- Dana Rondel

## Higher Truth Statements


*Higher Truth Three*

When we rise and reach greater and loftier heights in our lives, we allow others to not only see the splendid realities that we have made possible, but we open another window in life so others can see a more perfect reflection of themselves through us, and experience as well through us the brilliance of The Most High visibly manifested in the world. We become that reachable light that others can witness and experience as tangible when we are being our Greatest and Highest Selves...

- Dana Rondel

## Higher Truth Statements

### *Higher Truth Four*

I will become more than I AM. I will achieve more and more everyday because I know that I can. I will recognize only that which is good in myself, only that which is good in others; only that in all things and places that I know should live and grow... I will think only of that which has virtue and worth. I will wish only for that which can give freedom and truth. I will expect only that which can add to the welfare of the [people]. I will live to live more. I will speak to give encouragement, inspiration and joy. I will work to be of service to an ever-increasing number. And in every thought, word and action my ruling desire shall be, to enrich, ennoble and beautify existence for all who come my way.

- Christian D. Larson

*Words* *may become mental palaces*
*that will* *live* *forever, or they may become shanties*
*which the first* *breeze* *will carry away. They may delight*
*the eye as well as the ear; they may contain all*
*knowledge; in them we find the history of the past as*
*well as the* *hope* *of the future; they are living*
*messengers* *from which every human and super human*
*activity is* *born.*

-    Charles F. Haanel

# Introduction

It is such a joy to write this book. I am grateful for the idea of it, for the purpose of it, for the way it fulfills me and will fulfill others. When I first thought about what it means to really live and be inspired daily, my mind overflowed with visions of such a reality. I then began to take steps toward manifesting my personal dreams and career aspirations. As I took each step, regardless of how long or short they were, I repeated to myself, "Life is good." When we can say this often, "Life is good," we've reached a place in our lives where we are not only living the joyful visions of our imaginations, but we want others to live in the glory of their lives too.

I share this world with many, many people, so why wouldn't I want to ensure that our individual and collective realities are as bright as we can make them. When I encounter others, whether a family member, friend or someone I have yet to become more acquainted with, I want our interaction to be of the highest regard. Why shouldn't we smile at one another? Why shouldn't we find pleasure within the space that we are occupying and creating together? Why shouldn't we leave the experience, whether temporarily or permanently, feeling greater than we did before the experience? Why not allow ourselves to be open to—The Gifts of *Mind*?

As the Founder and Lead Minister of *Wisdom In New Dimensions (WIND)*, I am in a position to show others a higher way to live and be. So I decided that first, I have to live my own truths. I need to make sure that they are really working in my life the way I thought they would. I need to know and see for myself the magnificent realities that could and would come forth if I allow myself to be open to not only the truths that are taking root in my mind, but those that I came to learn about and witness through simply participating in the experience which Life is offering me. The truths that I can live with, really, really live with, without experiencing any doubts about them, are the ones that I fully align myself with. Those that cause me to question whether or not they are adding value to my life, I decide to move beyond. And when I do, I tell myself, "It's okay. It's my life."

Within my ministry and through my books, talks and other creative endeavors, I am offering others the opportunity to witness and experience a greater life based on the truths that have brought me personal happiness and career fulfillment. I love my life and am extremely grateful for the gift of service which creates a space for me to both give and receive. Reciprocity is a blessing of openness, a blessing that prospers when I am expecting nothing but allowing for everything I aspire for. The Universe is abundant. There will never be a time when we will not have what we want for ourselves. It all is always here, yet we must see it, even before it is physically visible and tangible. And we must hear the voice inside that says, "Trust the Omnipresent, Omniscient and Omnipotent Life that is everywhere, in all that exists, in all places, spaces and people at all times. Know that there can be only good for us and will be only good for us all, if we trust and know this truth without fear, without doubt, without worry. Trust."

Trust is part of the foundation, a stepping stone, of my ministry. There were times when I would take small, slow steps toward my dream and goals for *Wisdom In New Dimensions (WIND)*, and there were times when I would take large leaps of faith. It didn't matter which I did, what mattered is that I took the steps. I took the steps. Sometimes I looked back and wondered, "Am I going in the right direction?" I'm glad I asked the question, because the answer always came. That answer was, "Keep moving forward." I did. I took more steps, then more, then more until I was where I wanted to be, or until I reached a place I was destined to be. Even after getting there, I will admit, I would sometimes look back, but only to see how far I had come and how far one could go when they know that all is good.

My work as the Lead Minister of *Wisdom In New Dimensions (WIND)* is not only being done in our world, it too is being received. It is received by individuals all across life and it makes me ecstatic. As a leader of a spiritual organization (church), it is vital that others are able to embrace what is being shared. So I focus on conveying messages that are both universal and simple. I want people to know that it is okay to be who and what we are, and to believe who and what we believe, but accept as a fundamental truth for our lives that, life is meant to be fully lived, fully experienced and completely good. If we are not living the life we dream, experiencing the life of our greatest and highest thoughts and are not in alignment with the truth that good is always present, then ask, "What steps do I take now to get me there?"

"What steps do I take now to get me there?" I asked myself this question more than once. There were multiple responses that came, rather than just one. One of the more important ones was, "What do you require in order to ensure that your church maintains the integrity of its purpose and mission?" Hmmm… What do I require? I am not being asked, "What do others require…?" I am being asked, "What do you require…?" Wow. This is a powerful question. It is powerful because it places me in a position of authority and accountability. Does authority and accountability make the road longer and harder for me? It could. But for me, it didn't. It made my journey clearer, more beautiful and so much more enjoyable. I gained further insight about myself, about my abilities and most importantly, I learned my own power. I learned my own power.

The purpose and mission of *Wisdom In New Dimensions (WIND)* is to raise consciousness and to elevate souls through the creative and universal arts and sciences. I know that by raising the consciousness of people globally and guiding them toward increasing their self-knowledge they will become more aware of the expansiveness of their mental minds and intuitive insights of their hearts, which will allow for a more fruitful, love-centered and peaceful life. First, however, I had to do something more. It became necessary for me to not only speak to others about how *Wisdom In New Dimensions (WIND)* is different in its approach to fulfilling its endeavors, I had to show people. I had to make my church truly live up to its potential and show up to demonstrate its power.

Omniversalism came to life. It came into being to move both myself and others beyond older religious and spiritual paradigms into newer ways of thinking, living and being. Omniversalism is simply a spiritual pathway that roots those of us who travel this way in the truth: *God Is In All. All Is In God.* There is never a time when we are not fully connected to the Omnipresent, Omniscient and

Omnipotent Life. And though this be true, to fully acknowledge God as full, complete and perfect within us, we must know this truth in our own minds, confess it with our own mouths, witness it ourselves in all existence and live it through our daily deeds. So today, I live and lead with this truth in mind.

This book will share more of the truths that came to consciousness while traveling the path I am on today. These truths which in my mind are clear and simple have led me to a bright, beautiful and fulfilling place within myself and therefore, I am able to live the good within me without. As one is on the inside so shall his/her world be on the outside. Together, let's make it an even brighter world. My guiding light, the highest wisdom of my mind, is fully lit in order that you might too know and see a clearer and simpler way to God. *Rise and Reach* my friends. Live a life you dream. Lead a life of purpose. Are you ready? Since you are reading this book, I would say, yes, you're ready…

Welcome to the *Omniversal Life International (OLI) Life & Leadership Program.* Having this book means that you are taking the initiative, a step, toward a new life. During your reading you will be introduced to: *Life and Leadership Models & Strategies.* Enjoy them! Developing your insight and enhancing you is meant to be fun, but remember as you are moving forward, the following words:

> There is no labor from which most people shrink as they do from that of sustained and consecutive thought; it is the hardest work in the world. This is especially true when truth is contrary to experiences. Every appearance in the visible world tends to produce a corresponding form in the mind which observes it; and this can only be prevented by holding the thought of the [Higher] Truth.

> --Wallace D. Wattles

# Chapter 1
# Above And Beyond

*Take the first step in faith. You don't*
*have to see the whole staircase,*
*just take the first step.*

\- Martin Luther King, Jr.

Let's take another step. You have decided you
are ready to go above and beyond where you
currently are. As I smile, I am too applauding you.
Life is good. At this juncture of the journey it is
necessary to begin the process of releasing older
paradigms, ways of thinking, and be introduced to
new thoughts, ideas and positive affirmations which
will encourage us all and instill in us all the
confidence that is required as we each move
forward. With this confidence we will know that
regardless of what we hear—that is not in alignment
with our new way of thinking, regardless of what
appears before us—which shows itself as contrary
to the truths we now know, and regardless of what
might seem challenging—but in reality is only an
opportunity being presented to us, we will still
move forward. We will keep going because our

lives matter, our dreams are possible and because we can.

Knowing how the mental mind works is extremely vital. It is through our mental minds that our realities are created. What we think, we become and we experience. There's a term that I've heard others use, that I will share with you: *Think Good And It Will Be Good.* These powerful words benefit me tremendously. Just saying them aloud raises my level of thinking. They transform my life in the most glorious ways, simply because when I expect good, I receive good. If I expect anything less than good, I receive less than good. For many of us, good is relative, nonetheless, it's a term I am using for it defines for me our ability to live a life that brings us true happiness.

In the earlier pages of this book, I included four (4) Higher Truth Statements. They are Higher Truths that I have written and/or discovered and embraced and want to share with individuals who are a part of *Wisdom In New Dimensions (WIND)*, my global spiritual community, and those who are just seeking to know who we are as an organization and what drives our ability to create positive and lasting change in individual lives, our communities and the world at large. At this time, I am interested in re-introducing them. When you read each affirmative statement, reflect on the words being conveyed, meditate briefly to grasp the greatest understanding of them, and think about how they might move you to the next level of thought. As you do this, I will further expound on why I wrote them, why these Higher Truths matter to me and to the individuals who live by them. The order that you read and study each Higher Truth is inconsequential; however, I will share them according to their current order.

## Higher Truth One

Many believe in the Omnipresence of God (Spirit, Divine Love, Infinite Intelligence, Universal Creative Force, Allah, Jah, Jesus Christ, Yahweh, Brahman, etc.), nonetheless, it seems difficult for individuals to believe in the ubiquity of Good...If God is everywhere, at all times, then it must be the same for Good (God). In spite of appearances, circumstances, and present experiences, there is nowhere in life or in the world where there isn't Good.

- Dana Rondel

"Many believe in the Omnipresence of God..." What do these words really mean? The dictionary defines Omnipresence in this way: *Present every - where at the same time.* Let us further explore this.

There is no time when Divine Presence doesn't exist. There is no place, no space and in no person where Divine Presence isn't. This means that in life there is never a time when we are not experiencing the Omnipresence that is. If this is true, and for me it is, then there is never a time when we are not co-operating and co-creating with God. When we are co-operating and co-creating, we are conveying to the un-manifested (invisible) Universe in thought, words and deeds, through our affirmations and aspirations, that we want to create something for ourselves within the visible, tangible world where we currently exist. Do we really have the power to do this? Yes, we do. We have the power to create our own lives and our own realities. If we have the ability to manifest what we aspire for in our lives, why wouldn't we create for ourselves a life that is worthy of our own presence? Are we not, too, divine? We are divine. We are divine beings living a spiritually-human life. We experience mind and body simultaneously. The mental world (mind) is not separate from the physical world (body) within our earthly existence. Therefore, what we think, we become.

After the word, "God," I placed in parenthesis additional names that individuals, groups and organizations have used to identify the Omni-presence. I thought it necessary to do so simply because it allows me to surrender the idea that the

Omnipresence, God, can only be called by one name. It is not my relationship with the name of this ubiquitous Energy that becomes the driving force for my life, it is my relationship with Divine Presence itself that informs, inspires and moves my life above and beyond the existing notion of who I am and what I am capable of. In short, identifying with a given name may only allow for a partial experience with the Divine Presence rather than a full one.

"If God is everywhere, at all times, then it must be the same for Good." If God, the Omnipresence, is indeed the un-manifested, invisible energy in all life, that we have the ability to co-operate and co-create with without restrictions, without conditions, without questioning our intentions, then this Energy is a Divine Presence that is fully trusting, open and benevolent. Would we not then say, "God is Good?" I would say, not only is God Good but that Good is God.

"In spite of appearances, circumstances or present experiences, there is nowhere in life or in the world where there isn't good." How can God and Good be everywhere at all times, in all places, in all people and in all that exists when there are those in the world at large who see, speak about and experience suffering? In truth, we all are not at the same level of awareness within our lives. When I think about my own life, fully acknowledging the

Higher Truths took years of exploration, various forms of meditation and candidness—the ability to be honest with myself about what I really want for my life, as well as for the lives of others. During those years, I experienced what I thought were trials and tribulations. Through silence and stillness I found out I was experiencing or witnessing only what I feared. When a fear manifested as a tangible experience, it was simply mental energy, thoughts in my subconscious, being released. I could see my fear, I could feel it, and I could now know it more clearly. In essence, I was being offered the opportunity to make a choice about its place in my life. I could continue to develop a relationship with this fear or part ways with it. Move above and beyond it in order to see not only my life differently, but to see life itself differently. I could live the Higher Truths, which allowed room for only the thoughts, words and deeds infused with divine love—the unlimited, unconditional, altruistic energy of the Omnipresence, God. What appears before us, we perceive according to the thoughts in and conditioning of our mental minds, and yet we always have the choice to see things the way they really are, good, so that our greatest and highest perceptions become our life, our reality.

## Higher Truth Two

Our daily work is to prosper our lives mentally, emotionally (heartfully) and physically — holistically, so that we become fully connected with our Greatest and Highest Selves (Our God Soul), which then allow us to more completely realize our relationship with The Most High. It is our relationship with The Most High that opens up within us a deeper and stronger awareness of our truest potential as a Spiritual People — Full Beings... We, as Full Beings, then know without fear, doubt or worry that we can do all things through God who strengthens Us...

- Dana Rondel

"Our daily work is to prosper our lives mentally, emotionally (heartfully) and physically—holistically, so that we become fully connected with our Greatest and Highest Self, Our God Soul, which then allows us to more completely realize our relationship with God..." How many of us focus on all that makes us who we are—our breath, our dynamic, internal energy and the physical parts of our selves which allow us to more fully identify with the spiritual and tangible worlds we're a part of? Do you know the difference between your thinking mind (conscious) and your thought mind (subconscious)? Do you understand how both affect your entire life? Can your thinking mind and thought mind determine your emotional and physical states and vice versa? Let us explore these questions more.

There was a time when I defined my life by the convictions, ideas, teachings and words of others: family, friends, educators, mentors, writers, leaders, etc., and when I measured my life based on whether or not I successfully applied what I learned, which was for the most part determined by the facial gestures and/or verbal or written recognitions I received. Within this period, I didn't fully realize that the individual who I was and was becoming was not who I decided I want to be. Instead, I was and was becoming a person who others thought I should be based on *their* perceptions of life and the world we were living in. In summary, I was not living my life according to my own inner knowing and greatest perspectives. I knew I was capable of experiencing and seeing the world differently than others, but I didn't know that it was okay to live my own truths. Being different wasn't the norm, therefore, it seemed to make sense to follow the more common way even if internally I felt it wasn't the way for me.

Too many of us have let ourselves believe the common way is the easiest path to travel in life.

Perhaps for some this is true, but my own experiences led me to additional places, spaces and people who in one way or another encouraged me to question the choices and decisions I was making. Sometimes this encouragement was in the midst of what I perceived to be challenging circumstances. In truth, these circumstances were only windows of opportunity opening for me to further explore my current beliefs and ideas freely and the choices and decisions I made. A greater awareness was making its way forward in order that I could be introduced to a more mature mind.

Maturity leads us toward freedom. Freedom lets us discover more of who and what we are. For some, this walk could be frightening. For me, it is an adventure that I enjoy. I can't say that the adventure didn't at times make me wish I hadn't opened certain doors, but the beauty of every experience is that freedom is always present. We don't ever have to be stuck. Being stuck just like freedom is a choice. Which one do you choose at any given moment? The thought mind, our subconscious, awaits the answer. It receives from our thinking mind, our conscious, the instructions for the next step, therefore, it is vital that we share with our thought mind, our subconscious, only what we intend to create as our reality. To think clearly and creatively about our lives and the world we are agreeing to occupy is what I would call—positive thinking. When we are living a glorious life, full of peace, divine love, beauty and prosperity, I would say—we are living a life influenced by good, positive thoughts and constructive emotional responses.

Positive thinking and thoughts, and our emotional and physical states. To live a holistic life means we are of the knowledge that our mental minds, our conscious and subconscious, our emotional bodies, our feelings, and our physical bodies, our responses, are all connected. They are connected by the Omnipresence, the pure breath that moves throughout our entire being and throughout all of existence. To affirmatively acknowledge and speak about this connection is to convey, "I am perfectly healthy," which takes into consideration that, because the pure breath of God permeates my entire being, my mental mind, my emotional body and physical body, I can only experience perfect health. To experience other than perfect health is to experience lower, dynamic, vibrational energy stimulated by unfavorable external influences, disagreeable thinking, thoughts and feelings and/or unsound reactions. It is always wise to be cognizant about what we allow as our thinking and thoughts, which affect our emotional and physical bodies. It is too important that we choose to engage in only those experiences which will allow us to sustain our overall well-being of peace and joy.

To illustrate, a student is told by her instructor that she does not have the capacity to learn at a higher level because she has performed poorly in most standard high school subjects. The student allows this belief to become a part of her own thinking which then influences her thought mind, subconscious. Each time the student is required to take a test to graduate to the next school level she fails it. Because the student has internalized the words and feelings of her instructor, prior to taking any test, the student becomes insecure (mental/ emotional response) about her learning abilities, which affects her esteem (mental/emotional response) and causes her to become upset (emotional feeling/unsound reaction) and suffer from headaches (physical condition). The lower, dynamic, vibrational energy from the diminishing thinking and thoughts of the instructor have been transmitted to the student and therefore have adversely influenced the mental mind and emotional and physical bodies of the student, and so, has diminished her overall well-being and attitude (altitude).

In parallel, a student is told by his instructor that he has the capacity to achieve at any level regardless of past test results. The instructor continues to encourage the student by affirming her belief about the student's learning abilities. The student is positively persuaded by his instructor to study more and to believe in his own abilities although he knows that he has continually failed standard high school tests. The student studies more, his confidence and esteem is increased and he begins to garner higher grades. The instructor is pleased by the results of the tests taken by the student; the student becomes more disciplined in his studies, no longer shies away from taking tests, is capable of rendering an outcome that he is always happy with and no longer is affected by physical conditions associated with feelings of insecurity and low self-worth. Due to the instructor's life-affirming and uplifting thinking and thoughts, the student's thinking and thoughts, emotional feelings and physical behavior are healthy. The two scenarios shared are clear and simple examples of how our mental minds, emotions and bodies are connected and affected by dynamic, vibrational energy— energy that is transmitted by our thinking, thoughts, feelings, deeds and reactions.

"It is our relationship with God that opens up within us a deeper and stronger awareness of our truest potential as a Spiritual People—Full Beings... We, as Full Beings, then know without fear, doubt or worry that we can do all things through God who strengthens Us..." Whenever I am a witness to experiences like the one within the second scenario above, I am reminded of the power existing within our world and that is fully alive within our relationships. To motivate and move another toward an outcome that positively shifts their life requires audaciousness. What allows us the audacity to determine the way for another's life? What source fills us with inspiration and life affirming energy—an energy that has the ability to completely transform us? What gives us the inner strength and courage to walk a higher path of life and to encourage others to do the same? What declares for us that this path we have chosen is indeed a superior one? Perhaps for some the answer differs. Maybe for others they're inconclusive; but what cannot be denied by any of us is that our "Greatest Good" lives in us all as well as in our natural habitat; and that when we fully acknowledge and connect ourselves with the pure breath in life, our "Greatest Good," the meaning, purpose and mission of our lives become more clearly defined. We all may not call our "Greatest Good" by the name God or The Most High, yet when our awareness of this "Omnipresence" or "pure breath" becomes the guiding force in our lives we are then delivered into a life which allows us to more fully recognize our spiritual power and human potential.

## Higher Truth Three

When we rise and reach greater and loftier heights in our lives, we allow others to not only see the splendid realities that we have made possible, but we open another window in life so others can see a more perfect reflection of themselves through us, and experience as well through us the brilliance of The Most High visibly manifested in the world. We become that reachable light that others can witness and experience as tangible when we are being our Greatest and Highest Selves...

- Dana Rondel

"When we rise and reach greater and loftier heights in our lives, we allow others to not only see the splendid realities that we have made possible, but we open another window in life so others can see a more perfect reflection of themselves through us, and experience as well through us the brilliance of The Most High visibly manifested in the world. We become that reachable light that others can witness and experience as tangible when we are being our Greatest and Highest Selves..." To heighten one's own life, to be lifted by someone else's thoughts, words and/or deeds, to elevate another, is to experience a magnificent reality. It is a reality that brings us to the greatest and highest place within ourselves and allows us to witness the power and potential of the human life—its magic. Magic that I refer to as the brilliance of God. We all are capable of creating a brighter, tangible existence in our world. The wisdom we gain primarily from observing life, the knowledge we acquire from our participation in and exploration of the natural world and the understanding garnered through our intimate relationship with the ubiquitous, spiritual phenomenon that imbues all that is, are the bridges that connect us to our own divinity. Once we come to know that the human life is divine we become aware of God in everyone, in every experience and in all of our manifestations. This expanded realization that, we are the authors of our lives, co-operating and co-creating with God and with one another each of our experiences, tends to awaken us to not only the greatest possibilities and promises, but also to our significance and the significance of others.

## Higher Truth Four

I will become more than I AM. I will achieve more and more everyday because I know that I can. I will recognize only that which is good in myself, only that which is good in others; only that in all things and places that I know should live and grow... I will think only of that which has virtue and worth. I will wish only for that which can give freedom and truth. I will expect only that which can add to the welfare of the [people]. I will live to live more. I will speak to give encouragement, inspiration and joy. I will work to be of service to an ever-increasing number. And in every thought, word and action my ruling desire shall be, to enrich, ennoble and beautify existence for all who come my way.

-    Christian D. Larson

"I will become more than I AM. I will achieve more and more everyday because I know that I can." These words alone profess life. Their value is immeasurable and by themselves they can stand as the preface for the remaining lines of Christian D. Larson's affirmation. When we repeat these words to ourselves or say them aloud we are conveying to the thought mind, our subconscious, and the Universe, God, through our thinking mind, our conscious, that we are open to the greatest and highest possibilities and promises of life. And not only are we receptive to the intangible and tangible gifts of Mind, but we are extending our blessings to others, whether directly or indirectly, by coming forth as our Greatest and Highest Selves. As our Greatest and Highest Selves we are fully connected with the Omnipresence or what I have also referred to as our "Greatest Good." In this interrelationship, as noted earlier, we see only the good in every individual, every experience and all else that is. We become more and more familiar with this good as it is the primordial energy permeating our lives and that manifests in our lives. It is so because we acknowledge it as so. If at anytime we experience other than what we perceive to be good, we seek to understand the meaning of the entire experience and allow for the conception of an unbiased truth. This truth then presents us with the opportunity to transcend the experience by transforming and/or transmuting the energy—the seed and root of the cause. Our Greatest Good is the life, wisdom and power that motivates us to change our circumstances by moving above and beyond them, to change the appearance of things by seeing them differently and to change our life by expressing our own convictions and ideas about ourselves, others and our world. Our Greatest Good is life, wisdom and power. Life, wisdom and power are our freedom. Our freedom is a sublime and countless gift.

*God is Grand... Love is Divine... Life is Good...*

*Thank You God*
*for filling me with your life,*
*increasing in me your wisdom and power.*
*You are the air, heaven,*
*endlessly bathing my inner temple*
*and my outer earth.*
*My world is your playground*
*where the treasures in and of life are infinite,*
*the beauty in and of life eternal,*
*the magic in and of life abundant.*
*I will always follow Your Way.*
*I will always live Your Truth.*
*I will be Free, for Freedom is Harmony.*
*Harmony is Love.*
*Love is Breath*
*Breath is You,*
*Creator.*

-   Dana Rondel

# Chapter 2

# I See

*The world is a mirror*
*reflecting back my perceptions of self*
*and my perceptions of life.*
*How should I see?*

Some of us, if not all, have heard the phrase:
*Paradigm Shift*. The dictionary defines paradigm as:
*An example serving as a model*. The definition of
shift is: *To change from one ratio or arrangement
to another*. If we merge these two definitions most
likely we would come up with a clearer one that
might provide us with more insight into the
meaning of "paradigm shift." For instance,
*Paradigm Shift* is to modify or change an existing
pattern—way of thinking, doing or being—in order
to garner a new result, outcome or experience.

When I first heard the phrase, *paradigm shift*, I
was working as an Information Technology
Engineer for a Fortune 500 company. My role was
to design and implement software and hardware for
the organization's national and international
computer platform. I worked primarily in this

capacity during my thirteen (13) years at the company. Although, much of my time was spent relating to a computer, I too learned the importance of relating to the people around me. Others' perspectives mattered to me and to my peers and therefore influenced my team's perceptions, decisions and work ethic, what we put out and its quality: software designs, hardware builds, computer blue-prints and training documentation, etc. The choices and decisions my peers and I made regarding the company's continuously changing technology platform was a big deal to all involved. Together, my team, management, our consultants and our customers, decided the direction for our "Information Technology" infrastructure and plat-form. How we managed ourselves, our customers' input and our technical resources could determine whether everyone's jobs became more streamlined and simpler or more convoluted and difficult. Of course, experience and wisdom taught us all the joy of making decisions and choosing methods that would simplify our lives and the lives of others. To successfully achieve our goals and acquire the outcomes that would make us most happy, open and effective communication was key. Open commun-ication, which included, active listening, allowed for positive and transformative results.

During my fifth year, my company began to work toward changing its business identity. The overall purpose of this transformation was to better leverage our current customer base, to attract new customers, to provide more innovative quality services and to increase our bottom-line. The newest members of our executive staff thought we could best achieve each of these goals by working from the inside out, which meant we first had to overhaul the current corporate culture. The way things were being done had to be modified or completely let go of to fulfill both our tactical and strategic plans. Of course, this wouldn't be an easy task considering the size of the company and the fact that many employees, top-tier and bottom-tier managers grew quite comfortable with the familiar, internal culture, business designs, systems and routines. What we all understood was that, once something is learned and a process is created that allows for an easier and simpler way of completing a task, the existing methodology becomes the adopted and most times strongly embraced practice. Also, generally speaking, it takes more time and money to re-educate an entire organization, especially if it is a large one; therefore, our higher level executives and top-tier managers would continue to resist the recommended solutions offered until they could see for themselves, on paper and through case studies, how they could quickly garner a return on their investments and immediately profit from all of the changes that would be made.

One case study taught us the following and helped us to successfully implement the changes required to grow our company. Managerial staff and outside consultants, who were responsible for implementing similar changes for Corporation A, set forth to prove through financial data and research how newer business theories and re-branding would work and grow their business. Executives and managers in Corporation A, who were initially resistant, eventually bought in to the newer ideas for the company. Soon after, new hires were brought in, the software and hardware platform was updated and a new business logo and slogan was created. All would see the new brand that now represented the organization. The brand— the logo—was bright, it was colorful and it had life, but it didn't wake up or change the internal corporate culture. The company thought, after all the work that had been done and money that had been spent, they were finally where they wanted to be, yet in reality Corporation A was still aligning itself with old patterns that were no longer producing the results required to bring the company forward. Higher level executives were displeased, the newest members of management as well as the consultants were fed-up, several resigned and business continued as usual. Why did this happen? What was overlooked?

*Things are the way they are because*
*we are the way we are.*

- Zig Ziglar

If we stood Corporation A in front of a mirror, the tangible changes that were made would be visible to us. We could clearly see them. Placing this organization before its own reflection would be no different than if we were standing in front of a looking-glass ourselves. The physical changes we make to enhance our appearance would be noticeable. Even if the change was a small one most likely we would still notice it. The company saw the big changes and the small ones: new employees, updated software and hardware, the implementation of innovative applications, a new company logo, slogan and colors. There were even workshops and seminars that introduced both old and new employees and management to the new branding images and way of doing business. There was a tremendous amount of excitement initially, because all could *see* the modifications that had taken place; but no one could *feel* a real and positive difference in the internal atmosphere nor did anyone experience a shift in the corporate culture that had long existed. The business language was the same, similar ways of thinking remained, customers' expectations were not fully met and the company's bottom-line results barely peaked above the existing dollar amounts. What happened to the change that was to be made from the inside out?

Being privy, through the case study, to the information exchanged between management and others within and outside of Corporation A, my company had come to understand that the primary concern Corporation A was facing was the inexperience of top-level executives, management, employees and their customers to effectively and honestly communicate with one another. Mis-communication, lack of communication and in some cases no communication affected all and was influencing the entire culture of the organization. Someone needed to let the company's management know that open and effective communication was important and vital for healthy growth. Communi-cation creates perception, perception creates a reality and reality lives through further realities. Each reality may be slightly different but the seed of these realities is the same. What is that seed? It is thinking that produces a sequence of thought patterns which influence behaviors and manifest real-life experiences. For a visual, consider the process a flower goes through before it fully blossoms. It is first a seed (our thinking) that is planted in soil (our thought mind). If the seed, our thinking, is healthy and is planted in proper conditions (a sound thought mind) then it should produce a beautiful, fully blossomed flower. If the seed, our thinking, is unhealthy, whether planted in proper conditions or in an environment which does not allow for the essential resources for growth, then in most cases the seed, our thinking, will not produce the flower we wished for and expected. Our thinking can contradict the greatest outcomes that we actually want to create.

Corporation A included higher level executives who had come to the understanding that the organization's employees, those on the bottom-line, weren't as critical to the success of the company as those who were in top and middle-management. Higher level executives expressed to management that because their bottom-line employees have direct access to their customers they should automatically know what their customers required from them. This thinking led middle-management to believe that their staff required minimal training to effectively and efficiently service their customers. The training budget was cut, bottom-line employees received slim-lined training, they were unaware of the expectations placed on them by management and they serviced their customers utilizing the skills they had, which in many cases garnered unsatisfactory outcomes and poor feedback. Due to these results both bottom-line employees and their customers experienced high levels of frustration and stress. It was rare for bottom-line employees to share their feelings and customer concerns with management, simply because that channel had not been opened. And a relationship that would allow for the trust needed to initiate this opening had not been established.

*Yesterday I was clever, so I wanted to change the world. Today I am wise, so I am changing myself.*

\- Rumi

A paradigm shift had to happen. Working on the inside of the organization was necessary. On the inside the organization's staff: higher level executives, top and middle-management and bottom-line employees needed to change their thinking. Better results for higher level executives, top and middle-management, bottom-line employees, customers and the company overall would occur with proper communication. This communication needed to be reciprocal. First trust would have to be established. Either top-level executives, middle-management or bottom-line employees would have to initiate a conversation that would invite open and honest dialogue. Within this dialogue all staff within the organization, regardless of their positions, would gain the knowledge needed to more adequately manage their teams or customers, more effectively employ the processes of their departments and more efficiently operate the organization so that they could, together, move it forward. In short, the functions of each level of staff would be clearer, expectations would be fulfilled, customers would render positive feedback and relationships would sustain their health. The image and financial status of the organization too would improve. The new reflection that Corporation A would *see* of itself in the eyes of management, its employees, the customers and world community would be one that would make everyone happy. And happy is a good *feeling*. That's what I'm thinking...

A positive shift in thinking would change the pattern of the thought mind which would lead to clear and effective communication. Clear and effective communication would create openness and trust. Openness and trust would create satisfactory results and successful outcomes. Satisfactory results and successful outcomes would reflect a pleasing image of the company. Vital components of all businesses are its ability to represent itself well and establish healthy relationships. What allows for healthy relationships is healthy communication. Communication is that bridge that links us to information, and information provides us with the resources that feed us for the purpose of growth and prosperity. Re-source, simply means, to return to the source, our inner knowing and wisdom which guides us in the way of greater awareness. In essence, at the heart of every successful endeavor, whether seeking insight from within or establishing and building personal and professional relationships in the world at large, is open and effective communication. There is at no time in life when we are not witnessing in one form or another the acts of interchange and exchange—acts of communication. How thoughtful our communication is will deter-mine how wise our choices and decisions are. You know the rest...The input rendered, garners the output that will inevitably reveal itself in the mirror of our mental minds and in the mirrors of our outer world. You determine what you'll see...

*Communication is the fulcrum on which*
*the world goes round...*

# Notes

## WISDOM

*Increase in me that wisdom*
*which discovers my truest interest,*
*strengthen my resolution*
*to perform that which wisdom dictates.*

\-   Franklin

# Chapter 3
# A Simple Law

*Renew your mental mind…*
*Create a new experience…*
*Manifest a higher reality…*

Have you thought about your mental mind's purpose? Have you assigned your mental mind a role? If you have, what is its purpose and role? If you haven't, perhaps you should? Not everyone has taken time to think about the purpose and role their mental mind will fill. If more of us did we would ensure that our relationship with our mental minds is a healthy one. Wouldn't you want it to be, especially if you are requiring it to assist you in attaining your goals and building your dreams? Think about this more… What purpose and role do you want your mental mind to fill in your life? If you can't come up with anything it's okay. Your mental mind already knows its purpose and role. It knows that it exists to serve you; therefore, your mental mind obeys you and fulfills all of your commands.

Consider further your relationship with your mental mind. It is similar to any other relationship, except that your mental mind is an excellent listener, it is extremely loyal and it is always present. Your mental mind wants you to be happy because its familiar internal state is harmony. It is entirely open to receiving from you life-affirming thinking—requests, prayers, wishes and affirmations that will allow you to invariably experience health, peace, love, joy, prosperity and so forth... We are meant to thrive in this world. Live to live more, as Christian D. Larson alludes to. We were not born into this physical existence to die. We were born to further awaken our imaginations, to explore more our natural state of being and to bring added beauty into the world that we, collectively, are creating. Life is good. It continually displays this for us, therefore, we must see with new eyes every day and hear with ears that will receive without distraction that whisper letting us know that we are here, now, and that life beckons to us to come forth fully.

Come forth fully... Come forth and experience the world that we are creating. A world that invites our presence for it knows who we are. It knows our power. It knows our mental minds. It knows us because it is our thinking and imaginations that have made it. We look around and wonder how can I have made such a world? Is it me that has created all this good? Or you ask, is it me that has created this suffering? Our thought minds, our subconscious, reveal to us not only the thinking by our individual conscious minds, but the thinking by our collective consciousness. We each are co-creators of this world. It is a world that we all will inevitably share with others; therefore, our thinking requires discipline and accountability.

To think is to be thoughtful and reflective. It is a primal function of our lives that requires us to be considerate about our perceptions, for our perceptions, what we imagine and reflect inwardly and gravitate to outwardly become our life and our world. What experiences do we want for ourselves and for others? Does our thinking allow for these realizations? If not, do we have the discipline to focus our thinking toward what we intend to manifest? The answer is yes. Discipline, albeit an exercise of commitment, requires only one thing from us—fortitude. An inner strength that propels us onward regardless of what might appear before us or what we might hear. The voice that matters most is the one that delivers the soft whisper we hear when our thinking is silenced. It says to us, "Trust God anyway." Trust God anyway — the highest existence, intelligence and potential in our lives.

Accountability is not an option it is essential for our lives. It moves us to accept our part as the maker of our individual experiences and causes us to decide the life and power of what we've actualized. At no time are we not in a position of authority over our experiences unless we choose to relinquish this right. As I think about this further, it prompts me to consider the life I am choosing for both my individual and collective experience.

- What am I choosing to create for myself?

- Who am I choosing to co-operate and co-create with?

- What do I want for myself?

- What do I want for others?

- What do others want for themselves?

- What do they want for me?

I thought more about each of these questions. They are important questions to ask ourselves and to ask others, particularly those individuals who we frequently associate with, those who we are building relationships with and more importantly, those who we are building a life with. Therefore, rather than provide the quickest answer I could come up with for each question, I decided to think more honestly, yet simply, about these questions by searching within myself for the deeper truths in and of my life and existence.

- Who Am I?

- What do I want?

The questions, "Who Am I" and "What do I want?" helped me to summarize my answers for the preceding questions. My answers then allowed me to create life-affirming statements that will greatly benefit my life, if I live daily by their truths.

## Life Affirming Statements

*I am responsible for my individual life and manifestations. Therefore, I choose to build a life of beauty, prosperity and fulfillment.*

*I matter. My life matters, and so do the dreams I dream for myself.*

*I choose to use my thinking and thoughts to convey to the Universe (God) what I most aspire to create for my life and for the life of others.*

*I choose to use my words to more clearly articulate to others what is important to me. It is vital to me that my words inform, inspire and uplift those who I share this world with.*

*Honest, open and non-resistant relationships are what I attract into my life. Within my relationships ideas that I and others share are expressed freely and nurtured without bias.*

*Those who I meet on this spiritual journey have come to compliment my life and to assist me, working with me to manifest what I have imagined, so I choose to use my imagination to visualize only what will bring forth continued good.*

*I experience acceptance, happiness and abundance personally and professionally.*

*Individual dreams when merged bring about our greatest and highest reality.*

*I am always the best that I can be for myself and for others and others are always the best that they can be for me.*

*Life is reciprocal and therefore I choose to give only what I want to receive. I expect, without reservation, the greatest and highest at all times from every experience.*

*Life is good...*

The more we think life-affirming thoughts and speak positive and encouraging words the more we condition ourselves to expect the greatest and highest for our lives and for others'. To renew our mental minds is simply to no longer engage in thinking that does not serve us for the better and to let go of old thought patterns that contradict the life we really want to live. To create a new experience is to completely change our perceptions of ourselves, of others and the world. See and experience the world from a lens of beauty and prosperity, our living and unwavering faith in good, and allow your imagination to expand your vision into your reality. Our truest reality is that we are magical beings, powerful—we must not fear our power—and we each are the masters over our own unique destiny. Let's, however, journey through this life together knowing that our Greatest Good is always within us, welcoming us, sharing itself with us and urging us to be and become more of who we were intended to be—God's most glorious creations.

# Notes

*Do not conform to the pattern of this world, but be transformed by the renewing of your mind. Then you will be able to test and approve what God's will is – his good, pleasing and perfect will.*

- *Romans 12:2*

# Chapter 4
# Trust Yourself

*If you want to awaken all of humanity,
then awaken all of yourself, if you want
to eliminate the suffering in the world,
then eliminate all that is dark and
negative in yourself. Truly, the greatest gift
you have to give is that of your own
self-transformation.*

- Lao Tzu

What do you want? A great life? Are your thoughts great? Reflect for a moment on these questions. Yes, more questions. Explore your mental mind and present life. Go deeper into your subconscious to see what's there, what you notice with regards to previous patterns of thinking, and to release old thoughts. To transform your experiences and your life, it's time to think differently. Start by focusing your attention on only what is important to you. Nothing else matters except what is necessary for you to live a full life. We do not have to ask for this full life. It's already available to us, but we have to accept it by openly receiving it; and by giving it freedom to express itself in us, in our lives and in the world we are experiencing. Our thinking, our thoughts, our feelings and our actions must be aligned with this new and full life. To be aligned with our new and full life, we must begin to live in the way we want even if our current circumstances seem to be in the way of us doing so. Move your current circumstances to the side, move everything you are not interested in out of your way, and simply press forward as though your dreams are already real and tangible. What you want has to be real in your mental mind before it can be real in your life, your physical world.

Meditation, silencing and stilling the mental mind, and relating to harmony, is a great practice. It can open the way to a deeper serenity in our inner worlds. Meditation also allows for further insight which in turn moves us toward clearer thinking that is both intentional and focused. Intentional thinking requires us to know precisely what we want. It leaves no room for indecisiveness. Focused thinking lets us concentrate solely on the result we are seeking to achieve. Our attention becomes exclusive to the result in order to give more life to it. As we continually give life to our idea and/or vision, we will begin to learn the way to achieve it. Trust God and stay open and receptive to the way in which God is leading you. Trust God and trust yourself.

*Learn to keep the door shut, keep out of your mind and out of your world every element that seeks admittance with no definite helpful end in view.*

- George Matthew Adams

Trust God and Trust Yourself. We are one with God. The Spiritual Mind, the Omnipresent, Omniscient and Omnipotent Life, is also our mind —our Limitless Mind. God being Omnipresent also means there is no place within us where God's breath doesn't exist. And there is never a time when we are not expressing the divinity, the omniscient and omnipotent life that exists in and as part of ourselves. Think about the power in and of our mental minds—our thoughts are the seeds of creation. Consider our emotions—our feelings are dynamic, vibrational energy that colors our thoughts and give them substance and form in the real world. Examine more our bodies. How often do we have to tell them what to do? They are intelligent, physical designs that regenerate themselves, that complete themselves and that allow us to fully experience our pure and natural environments and world. God, the Omnipresent, Omniscient and Omnipotent life in and part of us all, is our spiritual mind and breath, inspiring us to live deeply, to dream bigger and to expect the greatest and highest experiences for ourselves. God is life giving—the vitality in our lives invariably reminding us that WE ARE ALIVE.

*...inspiration, the art of adjusting the individual mind to that of the Universal, the art of becoming a channel for the flow of Infinite Wisdom.*

-   Charles F. Haanel

Think about all I have thus far communicated. Write down any thoughts that come to mind, as well record on paper all that makes you unique and special. I've already shared our similarities and what connects and interconnects us all. As it has been said, "We are more the same than we are different." And yet, what makes us different from one another is also important. We are not here to live someone else's life, or to take on someone else's personality or identity, we are here to live our own lives and to know our own selves. The biggest contribution we each can make in life is to give the gift of self. But first we each must know who we are—the individualized self.

*This above all: To thine own self be true,*
*And it must follow, as the night the day,*

*Thou canst not then be false to any man.*

Who Am I? What words will you choose to describe yourself, your character and your individual life? Since reading this book, are your descriptions of yourself the same as they might've been previously? As you write on paper those words you think best describe you, remember this— trust yourself. The person who you believe you are; the person who you want to be, and the life you intend to live begins with you. We have the ability to think, imagine and feel, and therefore, the power to create. We must use our abilities and our power wisely.

*To live a great life, be a great person.*
*To be a great person, think great thoughts.*

Now that you have written a list of descriptive words you think best identifies you, it is time again to go deeper into your mind. Take a few moments to meditate once more. Allow your mind to move into a space of silence. Hear what thoughts surface. What's the nature of these thoughts? Are they thoughts that make you feel good or just the opposite? Are they thoughts that motivate you to move toward achieving your dreams and goals, or are they thoughts that are inhibiting you, discouraging you and keeping you stagnant? If any displeasing thoughts surface, ones that contradict those thoughts that lift you, release them. Don't address them, question them or debate with them. Don't allow them to begin a conversation with you. There is no reason for them to remain in your mind any longer than they already have. Simply, bless them with silence. Silence is one of the greatest gifts of the spiritual and mental minds.

If you are in a location or place that does not allow for a quiet space, it's okay. Your practice is not to silence what is outside of you, but to bring silence to the environment within you. What will best allow for this? Concentration. Bring your attention to something peaceful in your immediate surroundings. Once you find it, observe it briefly. In what ways does this object symbolize peace? Think about it for a moment. Then close your eyes. Keep a mental picture of this object in your mind's eye and release all thinking. Once you are able to keep your focus on this object only, see it slowly fade away. Shortly, there should be only a blank space within your mental mind. Let this space move you into the space of silence—which then becomes a blank canvass in which you can begin to create your life anew.

What we want in our external world first has to exist in our internal world. I have already shared this point, yet I am sharing it again because it is an important one—our thinking and thoughts are the seeds that create our realities. Our thinking is the internal workings by our mental minds which make for us a life that we'll love or not love. Which is the reality you choose? Do you currently love your life, or do you awake each day wishing for something different, or something more? Do you frequently look out on the world and wonder why God and/or humanity has allowed for so much suffering? Or do you walk out into a world that is serene and beautifully adorned with the myriad creations of Infinite Intelligence—the gifts of Mind? What makes you different from those who daily experience peace, beauty, joy, prosperity and all the greatest gifts in and of life? What makes you different is your thinking.

*I free from within me all that I have no intention on prospering. I internalize only that which I plan to build and make stronger.*

\- Dana Rondel

As you have learned, trusting yourself is important. To do so is necessary because you are the one responsible for your experiences, which become your life. You determine what thinking and thoughts, seeds, will be planted in your subconscious to create your ultimate reality. Will you allow thinking that contradicts what you have intended for your dream life? Of course not, for you are now taking the next step toward personal acceptance.

Personal-Acceptance, is a phrase I think will provide a clearer understanding of what it means to be the architect of one's own life. To better define this phrase, I first analyzed both words separately. The dictionary defines *Personal* in this way: *Individual or private. Acceptance* is defined as: *The act of taking or receiving something offered.* Considering these definitions, we can conclude that *Personal Acceptance* means: *To receive those relationships, truths, beliefs, etc. which can determine our individual experiences.* More simply put, whoever and/or whatever we choose to align ourselves with might possibly, partially or significantly, influence the direction of our thinking, therefore, the course of our lives. Knowing this allows us to discern more aptly our daily thoughts, feelings, choices, decisions and actions. Questions we might ask are:

-   Who or what is currently influencing my thinking?

- Why did *I allow* this person, truth or belief or these people, set of truths or beliefs to influence me?

- How has my prior thinking helped or hindered my progress toward my end result?

- When did my thinking create the end result I truly desired?

To best answer these questions, you must be in-tune with your own mental mind, your thinking and thoughts. It is vital that you are familiar with the source and/or seeds, thinking and thoughts, that you gave power to in order to initiate those experiences that became a part of your conscious life. Once you know the source and/or seeds, thinking and thoughts, responsible for your experiences, you can replace them, uproot them, transmute them or transform them into new thinking and thoughts that will render you more desirable outcomes. You have the wisdom and power to change your life by first changing your thinking and thoughts. There is one architect of your life—YOU. And God gives you all the resources you need.

# PERSONAL ACCEPTANCE

*My beliefs are my truths which build
a strong foundation for my life.
My relationships are those I have chosen
because they reflect the beautiful, honest and
harmonious relationship I have with myself.
I know that others' experiences are
not meant to be mine but theirs.
I know my experiences are not meant
to be others' but mine.
If I partake within a collective experience
it is because I have chosen to.
If someone else has chosen to become
a part of my individual experience
it is because they have chosen to.
Only I can choose to give power to
my thinking and thoughts.
Only I can be the Master over my mind,
the Architect of my creations.
Only I can live my life.
Only I can be Who and What
I am.*

# Chapter 5
# The Promise

*That a man can change himself,*
*improve himself, recreate himself,*
*control his environment, and master*
*his own destiny is the conclusion*
*of every mind that is wide awake*
*to the power of right thought in*
*constructive action.*

\-  Larsen

Allow only that thinking into your mental mind that lifts you to the greatest and highest heights within yourself and within the world you have come to know. Who doesn't want the greatest and highest experiences? I don't know many who, after achieving their goals and/or a significant dream, reached for nothing further or dreamed no other dreams. Yet there are those who simply just move with life allowing for the unexpected to transpire—this too is a beautiful existence. To expect nothing at all and still receive everything one could desire, or to expect the greatest and highest at all times and to succeed are both exalted realities. May we all live an existence that invariably brings us forward on the path of good will and good fortune. May we all want for others what we want for ourselves. The world is brighter when we all have our lights shining within it—intuitive minds awake with harmony, wisdom, love and beauty. How should we each ensure our part in this life and world? Think it, then envision your resplendent reality and know it to already be true. Feel it. To assist you on this journey, following are pledges that honor a glorious life.

## PLEDGES FOR A GLORIOUS LIFE

*I speak on only those things that I want: harmony, health, happiness and prosperity...*

Speak on only those things that you want: harmony, health, happiness and prosperity... The level of our thinking will determine the level of our speech. Our mouths convey to others the focus of our conscious minds. Do you choose to use words that are life-affirming? Do your words inform others by educating them with material that is useful to them? Do you use language as a means to inspire and uplift others? Do your words motivate you to move toward meaningful achievements? If you can answer, yes, to each of these you are consciously aware of the power in words. You know that language can change not only your life entirely, but someone else's, simply because words are in their truest form, thinking which holds within them a denser, vibrational element of sound. By speaking your thinking becomes more real. Words are the sprouts of those seeds in your mental mind. Choose and use your words wisely.

*I make all who come into contact with me feel that they are worthy of the greatest spiritually-human existence...*

All who come into contact with me are made to feel as though they are worthy of the greatest spiritually-human existence... When we come to know more about ourselves, who we are and what we are capable of, simply because of our relationship with the Omnipresent, Omniscient and Omnipotent Life, we begin to live as though we are worthy of a fruitful existence. We become more courageous and confident in our abilities to create only what we desire. We know that there is no limit to what we can do and what we can achieve. We know that only good exists and this knowledge inspires our fulfilling interactions with others and influences our experiences overall. As we continue to grow in our awareness of the indwelling life, wisdom and power we are endowed with, we become more astute in our thinking, we recognize and honor more often the brilliance that too exists in others, and our lives continually reflect a resplendent light which opens the way for others to follow.

*I remain optimistic and allow for this state in and of my conscious mind and being to be a stepping stone to the greatest and highest human potential…*

Optimism is a state in and of our conscious minds and a way of being which moves us toward our greatest and highest human potential... What allows for optimism? Our experiences have taught us that when our vision of the life we want remains clear within our mental minds, and when we are steadfast in our walk toward reaching a desired place there is nothing and no one who can deter us. Optimism also transmits to us that there is nothing or no one who is interested in keeping us from our goals and dreams, for the Omnipresence conspires with us as well as with others to bring forth the aspirations of our own conscious minds and hearts. At times, it may have seemed as though certain experiences contradicted this knowing, yet if we allow ourselves to look beyond that which a lower perception has brought forth, we will see that we are still on course and if we keep on we will reach our desired destination at the perfect time. Optimism also makes conscious the awareness that, there is sometimes a fuller vision than the one we have seen for ourselves, and if we trust this wisdom we will gain an even better life. Optimism is what maintains our knowing that only good will transpire and that we always have what is required to make concrete our vision and to fulfill our dream. Optimism also lets us know that as soon as we give forth our prayer(s), either in silent utterance or in audible words, our request(s) has already been met. We simply have to fully open ourselves to receive what we have asked for.

*I always expect the best from myself, from others and from life…*

Expect the best at all times… Life is both mysterious and magical. It has a way of surprising us by revealing to us wisdom that we were once unaware of, introducing into our lives people we never thought existed, unfolding before us places we had not yet found, and so on… The element of surprise allows for the mystery and magic that is pervasive in our lives, yet we may not always recognize it. Once we become open and trusting of our Greatest Good, the ubiquitous life energy in us and in our world, we free ourselves from the perceptions that may have clouded our thinking. Thinking that limited our ability to live uninhibited. What does it mean to live uninhibited? It means that your mental mind is free, your visions are clear and your imagination is healthy and has no boundaries. Life is simply a blank canvass on which you can create your world. It may look anyway you want it to. It may contain all you aspire for. It may provide you with everything that you require to live the greatest and highest life. To live your best life, you must at all times expect the best from yourself, the best from others and the best from life itself. Expecting the best is simpler when we expect nothing at all, for then we allow for the sundry surprises of this beautiful existence. Just let the good happen...

*I pray not only for my own success but for the success of others...*

Prayer is powerful and life is reciprocal. As we utter, silently or audibly, life-affirming words and rich requests we send forth a wave of energy that has within it the power to impregnate life with the seed of possibility. As we allow this seed to be cultivated within the soil of absolute faith, and as we take diligent steps which move us closer to our vision, we begin to see our prayer(s) unfold before us in concrete form. In time, we realize, what we only shortly before knew as an unformed energy. If by ourselves we are able to give birth to a reality that began as thoughts, formless energy, then imagine what we can do for and with others. Think of the power in our thoughts and words and their magnetism when we commune with like minds. The possibilities for our visions and dreams swell and flourish as glorious and living truths.

Life is reciprocal, therefore, pray not only for yourself, but for others and know that there are those in the world who too are co-operating and co-creating with God on your behalf. There are no secrets that can be withheld from the Universe, whether or not we release any utterances. God knows our innermost aspirations, and like a loyal friend will share what is necessary with others, who are willing to work as well to make the dreams we dream in this life come true.

*I live in the eternal here and now, I live for today…*

Our power is greatest in the here and now, so why not live for today? The here and now is an eternal blank canvas in life allowing us to create and re-create our lives in any given moment. The here and now offers to us the opportunity to choose exactly what we want to unfold within our most present experience. It is a space that makes available to us our greatest potential as a creator of life. Yesterday, nor does tomorrow, exist within this space, therefore, our attention toward what we aspire for, where we currently are, here, now is un-diverted. When our attention is focused on the present space of existence, we begin to know and see there are no limits to what we can create, there are only infinite possibilities. In front of the eternal blank canvass in life where the here and now dwells, we have the ability to experience ourselves as creators, and as the immediate recipients of the gifts of our creations. Now offers to us what is real, infinite life, in order that we can endlessly give birth to creation.

Here and now we can choose our thoughts, the thinking we will allow to enter our conscious minds. We can choose to release energy from previous experiences and only welcome into our internal world solely what increases us. Here and now we can determine what will exist for our lives and what will not. In the here and now silence and stillness beckon to us to let go of the noise that precludes our deeper relationship with Divine Presence—a relationship that extends to us the truest knowledge of our infinite life, wisdom and power.

Today is a tangible experience. An experience we can more closely connect to. Living within the here and now simply means that today is eternally in front of us. It therefore allows us to decide what will be real for us within every given moment. It as well allows us to determine what truth(s) will become the promise(s) for our lives.

*I let my life be a gift that blesses …*

Life itself is a miraculous gift. It is a gift meant to be experienced beyond our premature knowledge of who we believed ourselves to be during the earlier stages of our inner, conscious growth and under-standing. There is never a time when Life isn't calling to us, urging us to welcome into our existence the sundry blessings of our Greatest Good. Simply, we are here, now to experience our highest life, spiritual strength and greatest human potential individually and collectively. Already, we have accomplished so much. We've become recipients of infinite ideas, mastered inventions and have created worlds beyond our own. We are exceptional leaders of local and global communities, common people who perform random acts of kindness and give with no expectations in mind, and we are splendid individuals who contain within us a life that is solely ours to make visible and tangible. This life inside us, what will it look like once we've given birth to it? How will we relate to and experience it? How will others relate to and experience it? What story will our lives tell?

The story that my life tells has always been important to me for my life matters. I am here, now. Each day I have an opportunity to explore the beauty of my existence. To know what I am truly made of. The wisdom I've gained informs me that God is my loyal friend and confidant, our existence is interrelated and the world is our garden where we together share in the experience of creating exalted realities, joy and good fortune. In inquiring about who I am to myself, my knowledge has un- covered for me that I am a gift unto myself. I am the good I'd once sought in other people, places and spaces. I am the eternal wisdom which silence has unfolded within me. I am the greatest and highest reality that my quest for truth has led me to. I am the power I'd at times relinquished due to my mis-understanding of who I am. I am the courage that life reveals to me at each step of my subliminal rise. I am the truth that makes strong my constitution which builds the firm foundation of my life. I am the love that knows itself as divine. I am the peace that surpasses all under- standing for it is unchanging. I am the grace that meets every experience with dignity, integrity and confidence, for I trust the Omnipresent, Omniscient and Omnipotent Life. I am the inspiration that breathes life into my visions and dreams. I am the happiness that moves me daily to embrace this wondrous dance of life. I am the perfection of the The Great Architect and Master, God. I am who and what I am because I have been made so — a GIFT OF MIND.

May my courage and convictions be the gifts that too bless you...

*I am always receptive to wisdom, even if it is beyond my current understanding...*

I am always receptive to wisdom, even if it is beyond my current understanding... I ask to know and God reveals to me the knowledge. I ask for wisdom and God unfolds before me truth; yet there are truths that were once beyond my understanding. When we have yet to comprehend infor-mation that is shared, regardless of the vehicle in which it is delivered, insight leads us to explore further the data or message being conveyed rather than discard it. To do so does not mean that we accept another's truth as our own, it simply means that we respect another's truth as their own. Individually, we live unique lives that bring us down paths that may not be known to others. We come into our existence with the ability to align with learning explored and lived by others, those who are familiar and/or similar to us, and with the ability to engage what is new and might have not yet been discovered. Some of us were told it is rare to come by individuals who generally seek unchartered territory, but many of this kind exist. To meet such people it is necessary that we are open and welcoming of what is uncommon to us.

Our individual experiences were not meant to be the same albeit, we are more the same than we are different. We each interrelate with the Omnipresent, Omniscient and Omnipotent Life, which means we all have access to the same degree of life energy, wisdom and power. The extent to which we make use of what we have depends on our level of knowledge regarding the existence of such energy, and our understanding of our ability to co-operate and co-create with it. Those who know more about what they have, do more with what they have, and generally those who do more with what they know and have contain a higher level of confidence in their faculties. Wisdom lends to us this advice: sometimes less is more. Simply put, the more we make use of our spiritual power the less physical work is needed. This doesn't mean that no effort is required, plainly, it means our spiritual power creates for us a simpler way of producing what we intend and/or aspire for. Not only this, but we also come into more innovative ways of simplifying life overall.

To be receptive to wisdom offered by another allows us to relate to information rather than to react to it. When we relate to what is being conveyed we communicate that we are open and welcoming of the greater good that is intended through the thoughts, words and/or actions shared. When we react to what is being conveyed we might possibly place ourselves in a position of losing sight of the truth that was meant for us. A truth that we could very well benefit from; and/or a truth that invites us to expose a new perspective which could positively impact and transform others. If at any time truth revealed is beyond our comprehension, we are to simply ask for the wisdom to know that which was intended for us.

*Ask and it will be given to you;*
*Seek and you will find;*
*Knock and the door will be opened to you.*

\-    Matthew 7:7

Words are not always necessary. We open others to the experience of relating to us more easily by allowing ourselves to show rather than tell. Sometimes, truth does not require written or verbal language. Truth becomes greater when it is lived. Give others the opportunity to relate to your truth by demonstrating it through your life, your good deeds.

*I allow the door of my conscious mind to be open to only those who will cherish and respect my mind as I do...*

I have always allowed myself to be the recipient of a greater wisdom. Wisdom is a gift I cherish and respect. It is good judgment which provides me with the confidence to move my life forward, to see greater visions and to reach for a dream that seems unreachable. Good judgment says to us, trust Life. Know Life wants us to experience its beauty, its mysteries and its magic. It is forever unfolding before us inspiration that manifests itself in myriad ways, such as uplifting truths, poetic prose,

vibrant visions and harmonious occur-
rences. It is daily waking us up to realize
again ourselves as glorious realities. We are
imbued with an intelligence that has no
limit to its depth of knowing. We are
designed to be perfect reflections of God in
human form. The Great Mind has endowed
us with an abundant existence. Why would
we ever choose something less for
ourselves?

To allow a lesser knowing of who and what
we are and are meant to be is to subscribe
to a limited life. We are meant to be the
greatest gifts of Eternal Life, walking in the
path of infinite potentiality. Our ability to
rise and reach the greatest heights within
ourselves speaks to the accessibility of a
wisdom that is always existing. This lasting
wisdom is innately ours to deeply explore
and further experience. It is insight that
implores us to unfailingly seek the greatest
and highest life, therefore, encouraging us
to let nothing into our conscious minds, our
internal worlds, that would move us away
from the promise of God.

*I perform great deeds not for recognition but because I am capable, I am willing and because I have been blessed to do so...*

I perform great deeds not for recognition but because I am capable, I am willing and because I have been blessed to do so... To want to be recognized for our contributions is to simply state that what we do matters; nonetheless, our innate wisdom and humility lets us know that there will never be a time when our deeds will go unnoticed, simply because we ourselves are aware of them—I would think we are always conscious of what we are involved in. We will know what we are doing and why we are doing what we're doing. If we don't know time will inevitably let us know. Our truths are always brought to light. With this in mind, it is vital that we create truths, or experiences, for our lives that we'll always be able to live with, ones we can fully embrace and feel good about. To me this is the highest recognition we can garner for ourselves. A recognition which lets us know our true value and worth.

Our true value and worth are not measurable, they are simply reference points which allow us to acknowledge our thoughts and feelings regarding ourselves, and anyone and anything that is calling for our efforts and making use of our personal time. Any deed that we perform should be done because it is an action that brings forth into our lives further pleasure and good fortune. A deed should not feel as though it's work nor should we think of it as work. I am not saying that work isn't worthy of appreciation, I am saying that when we live our passions and true purpose we will conduct only those tasks that extend our love and not create for us sacrifice. Great sacrifice has rendered for many, glorious recognitions, but great love has garnered for more, a deeply fulfilling life. If I am asked the question, why do I do what I do?, I hope I can always say, I do what I do, in the way that I do it, because I am capable, I am willing and I have been blessed to do so. I truly love what I do, and therefore, what I do lifts me into heaven within myself and within our world; and this is truly an honor that I myself will always recognize.

*I will always be true…*

I will always be true… True to who and to what? The answers for us can vary. I have already stated, we each live unique lives, and therefore, our perceptions, our truths and our experiences might possibly defer. With this being said, I would suggest that we each consider the wisdom we have acquired thus far. Who would you think of when you contemplate what is most important to you? What would you think of when you reflect on your experiences? Perhaps my answers could provide you with additional insight.

I will always be true to myself first and foremost, for to be true to myself is to be true to Life itself. And to be true to Life is to be true to our Greatest Good, the Omnipresence, which is in all and that all is in.

I will always be true to my visions and dreams, simply because they are those visions that add more color and music to my thoughts, and those dreams which provide substance to experiences meant to further fulfill me.

I will be true to my relationships for they are like the springs of water in a beautifully architected, stone fountain; they continually add life to the life that already is.

I will be true to the world of my own imagination, for in this world will exist only what I would intend for my most fulfilling life, and for the life of every woman, man and child, and for all else that inhabits it.

I will be true without regard to anyone or anything, simply because to be true is to be real and I am real.

I will be true for I am true—a truth I can live with.

I will be true simply because I can...

I will be true...

I will be...

I will...

Intuition

*Intuition is a spiritual faculty
and does not explain, but
simply points the way.*

-   Florence Scovel Shinn

# Chapter 6
# At The Top

*I know for sure that what
we dwell on is who we become.*

- Oprah Winfrey

Who and what do we will to be? Some will find this question easy to answer, while others will take time to answer it, mostly to ensure that their answer is a deeply thought out and honest one. Do any of us really know who and what we want to be? Do our answers change as our knowledge increases and as we gain more wisdom? Is it necessary that we define ourselves, or can we live more completely by simply and regularly being the fullest expression of our greatest and highest spiritually-human selves? What does this really mean? It means that we are now aware of ourselves as a complete embodiment of God, personified. We have all the qualities and characteristics of the Omnipresence, therefore, it is not necessary to add anything more to ourselves. All that is required of us is to explore and experience life further. To do so we'll need to choose paths in life which will most interest us and bring us increased happiness and good fortune.

I love to be inspired. My experiences have made me aware that others love to be inspired too. I found that, although there is much which has brought inspiration into my life, words, written and verbal, seem to have a significant amount of influence on me. Shortly after coming to this conclusion, not long after I graduated from college, I began to keep a journal which I used to record my new ideas and poetic truths. I also started to read more, mostly books that motivated me and encouraged my deeper discovery of the power in words. Whenever I became moved by words, written or spoken, I would announce to myself, "I am going to be an inspirational writer and speaker." The idea always awakened in me a smile and it increased my drive toward fulfilling my dream.

At the time I realized my true passion and life purpose, I was beginning a lucrative career in the computer science and software engineering field. Albeit, I knew without any doubts in my mind that becoming an inspirational writer and speaker would bring me lots of joy, I still liked working in Information Technology. As I continued my computer career, however, I attended symposiums and conferences where I would have the opportunity to hear live motivational speakers, I registered for creating writing courses at a nearby

University and I continued to keep a journal. Eventually, I decided to pursue my Master of Arts degree in creative writing and dance part-time. Yes, dance. I began my training as a dancer during the age of four (4), headed a dance ministry at my church after college, was asked to audition for a Broadway musical in my early twenties, which I didn't take seriously enough to pursue, and I considered opening my own improvisational dance and movement company after receiving my post graduate degree; but my enthusiasm in becoming an inspirational writer and speaker never dissipated. So I released the notion of becoming a professional dancer and instructor and focused on writing my first novel which would launch my full-time writing and speaking career. Today, several years later, I am still an inspired writer and speaker; I am further discovering the power in and influence of words, and I am living my passions and life's purpose. I have also opened myself more to the idea of doing whatever brings me additional joy and prosperity.

My love for writing and speaking remains strong. Words for me are a gift to inform, inspire and uplift. To more easily associate myself with these endeavors, I convey to others that I am a writer, author and orator; nonetheless, I do not use these titles to define my life, I only use them to provide information about what I do. In short, who I am is not a writer, author or orator, although writing and speaking are what I do, but I am an individualized expression of the Omnipresence, full embodiment of its life, wisdom and power. I am a spiritual-human being whose passion is unlimited and whose life's purpose is un-inhibited by any prior choices I've made or by any paths I've previously chosen. Life always beckons to us to live so that we may live more, consciously and freely.

To more fully experience the Omnipresence through our lives we must recognize ourselves and others as free. We must let go of any pre-conditioning or learning we've used to acknowledge who and what we are, particularly if we defined ourselves and each other by age or physical growth, skills or capabilities, titles or labels, status or recognitions, nationality or skin color and hair type, or by our educational experience or current knowledge, for we each embody eternal life, infinite intelligence and the greatest degree of spiritual potential, albeit we all are not yet aware of our real selves. The more we begin to open ourselves to the life, wisdom and power that is inherently ours to experience, the more we come to know about who and what we truly are and about the endless good we are capable of. To be open we must make the choice to live un-restricted by prescribed and/or self-definitions that could never thoroughly grasp the enormity of our greatest and highest selves.

It is important that we, as often as possible, find the time to still ourselves to relate to silence. Silence is like a wise teacher who speaks no words and yet is able to direct us toward the knowing that informs our lives. In silence we are capable of reaching the highest pinnacle of existence which allows us a more meaningful relationship with the Omnipresence. In this relationship we just are. There are no expectations of us except that we trust the experience which will ultimately render to us an unfathomable education and burst of inspiration. It is in silence that we first come to know and feel that we are truly one with God.

Creative power is at its greatest in silence. In silence our minds become undisturbed by distracting inner stimuli and external noise, energy which seems to dissipate the life of our interconnectedness with the Omniscient and Omnipotent Source. To hear the silent voice in wisdom we must release all noise, including lower thoughts and unclear thinking. To experience the unfelt strength in power we must do away with all distractions, particularly contradictory perceptions which divide our attention. Silence allows for the concentration that centers our conscious minds, moving out of them all that is not proprietary. When we are again experiencing our innate states in our physical forms, we are fulfilling our greatest potential as spiritual-human beings. We are the mighty vessels of God, reflecting internally and externally the ideal life. God first, and all other worthy and honorable aspirations of our sublime minds and hearts will come unto us.

It already is. There is no need to create what already is: perfect health, happiness, divine love, a prosperous and abundant life. Know them to be so now and they will be so. All that is required from us is to fully acknowledge and experience them. What live in our internal and external worlds are alive because we first made them real in our conscious minds through our thinking, our thoughts and our imaginations. Nothing can exist unless it first exists within our mental minds. If an experience has already been created that is undesirable, simply begin to focus on only what you truly desire. Give the undesirable experience no more of your time or attention and it will shortly fade away. Is it this easy? God, the Omnipresent, Omniscient, Omni-potent Life, is the only power. There is no energy existing in our internal or external worlds greater than the power of God. When we focus our attention on the perfection in, and beauty and prosperity of existence, which includes our own lives, we are acknowledging the life, wisdom, power and goodness of the Omnipresence. In this acknowledgment, we agree that nothing else can become real except what is already real—

perfection. God is perfection. The Divine Life is perfection. There is no need to utter the words, "It doesn't exist." Simply just recognize and honor what is sincerely and presently true—life reflects for us only what is real and perfect—GOD. And yet, only we can modify our perceptions to see this absolute truth.

When we are living as divine beings, experiencing only our Greatest Good—what is real and perfect, we then have arrived at the truth—there is nothing to resist. There is nothing to resist because every experience is a desirable one. Ones that offer us continued peace and pleasure. Worry, doubt and fear become non-existent, for we are now Masters over our conscious minds and Architects of our world. We create only what we know to be truths we can live with harmoniously. These truths become our actual experiences which provide us with insights that spur us forward to create the greatest spiritually-human existence with more beauty and good fortune. Our perceptions unfailingly reveal to us what a conscious and fulfilling life entails. We never grow bored of our experiences for the Infinite Life continually unfolds before us new worlds and more pleasures, new ideas and greater inventions. Life is in motion and it means for us to be invariably moved by it.

Intuition lets us discern more deeply what is true. Our intuition is keen and quick and provides us with facts which move us in a direction that is clear. When our direction is clear we are more apt to make the most sound choices and decisions for our lives. Consistently making choices and decisions that greatly benefit us and add more value to our existence lets us partake of the delight in life's playground, where our relationships are wondrous and gratifying and where bliss and amusement are inevitable. To develop our intuition we must exercise our inner eye. It is the eye in our conscious minds that sees before we are able to physically see and that knows before we consciously know. It alerts us to the stimuli around us, whether seen or unseen, heard or unheard, and gives us insight into the miraculous design and abilities of our intellectual bodies. Through the inner eye, our intuition, we are capable of experiencing worlds beyond our physical worlds and experiencing relationships beyond the ones in our immediate environment. We come to know and feel ourselves more truly as omnipresent beings. The natural atmosphere seems more like an extension of our lives rather than being separate from our lives. As a flower unfolds before us the unfolding of emotions in our un-fleshly hearts too gives way to life. As the blades of grass are moved to dance by the shifting winds we too can feel the lightness and resilience in our own selves. As the tides of oceans become still and calm we too feel that peace within us. As the heaven of God pervades our material earth we too feel the eternal height in life within our own forms. We all are extensions of not only Nature and all the splendid arrangements and living things within it, but we are also extensions of one another, for we share the same air, our eternal breath. We are here, now, as omnipresent, omniscient and omnipotent human beings. Our intuition opens the door to this glorious insight.

We have made it to the top. Each conscious step we chose to take, motivated by new information, innovative ideas, fruitful efforts and conscious discipline, got us here. We have earned our place amongst the brilliant bodies who first lit the way for us as we searched within ourselves and within the outer world to find our own bright lights. Now that we reflect the wisdom in our greatest and highest selves, and have the power to build our mansions upon the clouds in the sky and on the strong foundation of our lands, we may decorate them as we choose; we may experience them as we like, and we may invite those who too are willing to partake of the delight in life's playground. Let us all enjoy the experience...

*Thy will be done.*
*God's way is clear and simple.*
*Let us not cloud the highest vision and dream*
*for our lives with unclear thinking and noisy*
*thoughts.*
*Our imaginations are meant to soar,*
*not to be fettered by heavy perceptions of life.*
*Our sublime minds are free like a bird when*
*our perceptions are light with the beauty of our*
*truths.*

\-    Dana Rondel

# Chapter 7
# Creating Opportunities

*The longer we are able to hold positive thoughts in our minds, the more powerful the positive energy around us becomes. We don't need to focus on action and controlling so much when we are surrounded by energy that draws what we want toward us. We can simply respond to the opportunities that naturally come our way. When this is the essence of our experience, we can go with the flow, knowing that we will be okay.*

- Unknown

Opportunities are ceaseless, possibilities are infinite, our intelligence and abilities are enduring, and Life is a garden of endless landscape spread out before us to make use of. Our ideas, which become our visions and dreams, are seeds awaiting cultivation in this garden. Great and innovative ideas when fully blossomed deeply benefit our lives and the lives of others. And they create for us more opportunities. At no time and in no place are we not met by experiences and encounters which spark our inspiration and our inclination to move life forward. How do we actually move life forward? By opening ourselves to the brilliance that seeks to come through us.

There are no mistakes, there are no accidents, there's simply a creative force in existence which inevitably materializes what our conscious minds are able to conceive. Think about this. What thoughts first come to mind? Are they thoughts that remind you of the depth of our knowledge and power? Are they thoughts that make you wonder about the extraordinary experiences and encounters you have? Are they thoughts that delight you? The thoughts that come to mind should greatly encourage you. They should further motivate you toward maximizing the potential of your ingeniousness. The spectrum of our imaginations is immeasurable and our resourcefulness is unlimited, and therefore, I am continually led to search my creative mind for the next artistic and joyful experience which will add further value to my overall existence and to that in the world at large.

Inspiration is one of the most splendid gifts in life. It informs us of the magnificence of the Omnipresence; it empowers us to take leaps of faith and to trust that our landing will be on solid ground;

it moves us to take another step and then another
toward what we aspire for; it lifts us over that which
might seem to be in our way and urges us to keep
going forward, and it breathes into us the will to go
beyond our sleeping states to awaken to a sublime
mind anew and filled with a fortuitous outlook.
Inspiration is a treasury of illuminated promise
meant to fortify our lives. It is as well the spark of
light that encouraged me to found and build my
church, *Wisdom In New Dimensions (WIND)* and
my publications and media business, *Partners In
Goodwill.*

When I first began my full-time career as an
inspirational writer and speaker, my focus was
primarily to write books and to share their messages
at various engagements I would be invited to speak
at. Previous writing and speaking experiences led
me to believe I was good at what I did and that I
had the ability to deeply touch peoples' hearts and
positively transform their lives. My life-affirming
words, written and spoken, left lasting impressions.
I truly found so much joy in this knowing, in the
process of writing, holding completed manuscripts
and books in my hand, and delivering their inspiring
words that all I could think about was, how can I
create more opportunities to do what I sincerely
love? When I asked myself this question, ideas
immediately started to flow one after another. I
began to write essays and short stories I could share

with others weekly to further introduce myself and my work; I created community initiatives that addressed what others perceived as issues but what I saw as open doors to explore new possibilities. I partnered with organizations that focused on building the lives of children and families and further enlightened them on our spiritual strengths and human potentials—in order that we, individually and collectively, no longer associated ourselves with thinking that oppressed us rather than lifted us. I attended retreats with others who were in my field of work and who I believed would encourage my endeavors, and I hosted public talks and seminars that would allow me to grow my relationship with those who might be interested in hearing what else I had to say. All of these activities further expanded the realm of opportunity in my life. The number of individuals and communities, nationally and internationally, who wanted to know more about what I thought regarding our innate abilities to move our lives and the lives of others forward grew.

Books were one way to reach people. Public talks were another way, but not everyone would read a book and not everyone could make it to a scheduled engagement, and therefore, I had to find other means to connect to the world. And I had to discover how to afford others the opportunity to experience inspiration not only through words, but through other media and most importantly, through their own lives. My publications and media business came to life and my slogan for *Partners In Goodwill* became: *What Inspiration Sounds and Looks Like.* When we hear spoken words or see a reflection before us, whether our own or another's, I want us all to be able to say, "I am what inspiration sounds and looks like."

There are so many stories I can share regarding those who too expanded existing opportunities, or who simply came into an innovative idea that broadened the horizon of their lives and the world. During my travels, I've had the pleasure of meeting these special people and they come from all walks of life. Before I tell more about them allow me to remind you of those individuals who used their insight to build structures like our ancient pyramids, which gave us a glimpse into the genius in and of our early architects, of those who were able to articulate for us the medicinal properties and uses of the elements found in our inorganic and organic environments, of those who could display for us a way to brighten our world through the properties of fire and vital energy currents, of those who captured vibration, color and tone, to make music that bring us joy. Do you remember people like those who explored for us sundry ways of utilizing food like peanuts and sweet potatoes to create hundreds of other recipes? How about those who designed for us bathtubs, showers and other amenities which provide us a more efficient and convenient way of life? What about those who figured out how to bring us across neighborhoods, communities, nations and the world in the sky, through our water and on ground, and those who brought us closer through our airways and landlines? The list of expanded opportunities, innovative ideas, imaginative inventions and brilliant, independent thinkers are never-ending. We all have the same capacity to envision what has yet to be unearthed by another clearly for our advancement, comfort and pleasure.

As I write this chapter, I am reminded of a friend I met during my initial stay in Clearwater Beach, Florida. He is a man who runs his own cab service and who believes that his purpose is plainly, not just to provide individuals with a way to get from one place to another, but also to give people an experience that allows for a unique and fun journey. With this in mind, he decided to decorate the interior of his caravan with a disco ball, a flashing strobe light and other neat treasures and trinkets. While on the ride you become moved by songs that lift your spirit and entice you to sing along. If music is not something you desire, then Moses, the owner and driver, invites you into an informative and friendly conversation with him. He is not a man who was born in America and yet his experience here, mostly as a professional and celebrated cyclist, and his secular views allow us to travel with him through worlds that are familiar to many of us and to worlds that may be new. Moses, too, is quite tuned-in to people, so if nothing else he will remind you that life is meant for us to live moment by moment in order that we might not miss out on the gifts always present before us. His company, The Party Cab, slogan is: *You Got To Ride It.* I believe what he is conveying is that you got to ride the motivation that picks you up, lifts you to another height within yourself and that moves you onward, for life is continually worth living. Moses wants us to enjoy the ride of our lives regardless of the cost. We can afford it, and we are absolutely worth it.

Moses' story is just one. I have befriended a chef who opened his own restaurant in order to give people an eclectic experience with food, for he has had the opportunity to travel across continents and mix wonderful ideas that become delightful recipes. I've personally met a young and vibrant vocalist and musician who, through her intimate relationship with instruments, has brought humanity to new realms. I've also met many other gifted vocalists and musicians whose signature of song could not be paralleled, therefore, leaving us listeners with an experience that freed us from ourselves. My journey as a writer has also brought me into the company of entrepreneurs who patented ideas that made business processes simpler and professional relationships stronger, of ministers, bishops and archbishops whose words by themselves have spiritually fed and satisfied those who were hungry for new ways of seeing themselves and seeing our world, of athletes whose physical prowess seemed unmatchable by others but comparable to the greater forces of nature. I have met and befriended artists whose imaginations could not be bounded by what seemed unimaginable to others. I've met teachers and principals of schools, colleges and universities who despite the traditions of learning, went beyond old paradigms to introduce their students to newer dynamics of life—ones that exposed to students how to build worlds of their own rather than to dwell within a world already made. My life has been significantly improved by the lives of phenomenal friends, acquaintances and strangers who chose to defy limitation by embracing freedom and change. It is our freedom and change that has led us to our most valuable discovery, one that surpasses all others—the discovery of the vastness and splendor in our own creative minds.

# Notes

*Doing your best at this moment*
*puts you in the best place*
*for the next moment.*

– Oprah Winfrey

# Chapter 8
# An Abundant Life

*Seek the Kingdom of God above all else,
and live righteously, and God will
give you everything you need.*

- Matthew 6:33

Seek the Kingdom of God above all else, and live righteously, and God will give you everything you need. What does this mean? In previous chapters, I shared higher truths regarding the existence of the Omnipresence. These truths acknowledge that God is in all and we all are in God. There is no place where God isn't. There is no person in whom God doesn't live. There is no time when God doesn't exist. God being everywhere, in all people, at all times constitutes the ubiquity of Divine Presence, but more precisely these truths establish for us that the life, intelligence and power of God are invariably permeating our internal and external worlds. To be acquainted with such knowledge is empowering, yet to make use of this knowledge is to allow for a deeply and positively transformative and rewarding experience.

When we've found within ourselves the Kingdom of God, or what is also known as the essence of life, which fortifies our beings with breath, brilliance and influence we have come into a well-spring of everlasting riches. These riches, when properly utilized, garner for us a more ideal existence—one that in every way provides us with all that we'll ever need and more... Our fountains of life will constantly overflow and abundance is all that we will ever know. The whisper of Infinite Truth will declare this to our ears by conveying: I AM GOD. GOD IS LIFE. LIFE IS ALL. WE ARE ONE.

*I AM Omnipresence.*
*I AM The Way,*
*I AM The Testament,*
*I AM The Life.*
*Let not your heart be troubled;*
*YOU KNOW WHO I AM – Omniscience,*
*therefore you know Lasting Silence*
*and receive from it its Wisdom*

*YOU KNOW WHO I AM – Omnipotence,*
*therefore you know Eternal Life*
*and experience from it its Power*
*and allow for it to bless you*
*now and forevermore.*

The greater command for our lives as we are endowed with the wealth of God's Kingdom is to live righteously. To do so is to live a good and honest life. A life that exemplifies our greatness and that magnifies the transparent beauty of our individual and collective experiences. It is the path of virtue. The path of virtue is not a life lived under the microscope of judgment, but a life that moves us to further explore the limitlessness of altruism, to exalt our highest potentials as humanitarians, as we also allow others to witness God's benevolence and magnanimous love. God is the Way. The Way is integrity and charity.

God is The Testament. The Testament is an unequivocal truth. A truth that demonstrates the soundness of the greatest and highest character and will. Our sacred texts share with us: Your Kingdom come, Your will be done, on earth as it is in heaven. – Matthew 6:10. The explanation for these words is, what we inherit in the Kingdom of God, eternal life, infinite intelligence and limitless power, which are the gifts of a clear, silent and harmonious mind, the experience of heaven, will too be the blessings bestowed upon us here on earth. As the recipients of the universal, all-knowing and all-powerful energy of God, we transcend the limited perceptions of ourselves and others and then are able to witness and experience the enormity of our potential as divine beings. The Promise of God is fulfilled—the grand and immeasurable treasures of our inner worlds are experienced by us here on earth. In essence, God's character and will are made apparent through us in the material world, making us living declarations of God's Testament, the Highest Truth.

I AM REAL. This revelation gives breath to the words, God is The Life. As God is Life it is only God who can give life. God is Omnipresence, the Source of all good that is seen and unseen, heard and unheard, formed and unformed. Science and religion share that the innate, unchanging state of Omnipresence reflects the equilibrium of an endless and tranquil body of water. We are also aware that water is an ubiquitous energy existing in all life. Water as we know is visible in its liquid and solid states but invisible in its gaseous state. It produces sound we can hear when its motion is stimulated by outer forces and wind currents and it becomes quiet and calm when undisturbed. Water is also shapeless but can take on the shape of any object. It is one of the least resistant elements in our natural world. Like God it is benevolent.

We've been informed that our bodies are seventy to ninety percent liquid, and yet there is in no part of our physical bodies where water is not contained. It lives in significant amounts within every fiber, cell and particle of our being whether visible to us or not. If this were not true that part of our forms where fluid-water has evaporated would not degenerate. Even our bones have within them a high quantity of fluid substance which allows for their resilience and regenerative nature; otherwise they would become dust, which matter-of-factly is a change in form due to the lesser degree of water content or liquid moisture within. Our physical forms, like the earth, are bodies of fluid-water that is forever renewing itself. To keep the water in our bodies pure and plentiful, and to ensure the cleanliness and care of our natural environments is recurring, is to adhere to the inborn intelligence and constructive qualities in life.

What we currently know is that water is not only boundless in our natural environment, existing everywhere and in all people and things, we also are aware that it too has intelligence, is acquiescent and is life-giving. Now let us imagine that water, wherever it exists, unfailingly abides to its inherent, serene disposition, reflecting for us the harmony of God. Let us too allow the peace that pervades heaven to fill our earth.

God is The Life. The Life is Breath. Breath is eternal, pure and harmonious. If it perished so would life. When we consider Breath as eternal, pure and harmonious, we acknowledge it as time-less, organic and static energy or air. Static does not mean that air contains no activity, it means that its motion is at a rate of speed that is so fast its movement appears to us to be still, soundless and invisible. It is this Life that permeates all that is. It is alive within both our internal and external worlds, in our unseen and seen environments. The qualities of this timeless, organic and static energy, known as Breath (Air), are unparalleled, and yet water expresses similar characteristics. When water is in a gaseous state it becomes air, less dense and invisible to us, yet still living and functioning as an intelligent element in life. In its denser, liquid state, water feeds us, replenishes us and strengthens and builds us. When it becomes depleted, as a liquid, from our bodies or from any other form of material existence physical regression begins. If water can contribute to and increase our physical existence, we can only imagine the depth of our abilities as our awareness of God, our Eternal Breath, expands. Our abilities are immeasurable.

Prior to our enhanced insight about God, our Eternal Breath, most of us knew ourselves as only physical human beings, separate from the spiritual world. We understood we have material brains and to learn anything they must be used, but whether or not we comprehended how to use them was another matter. Our visible brains are the corporeal parts of our mental minds, our conscious and subconscious. Our brains' function is simply to receive by subliminal thinking (air) information primarily gotten through our physical world and senses, such as the sound of a piano's keys, the color of grass and trees, the smell of flowers, the taste of fruit and the feeling of degrees of temperature. The interaction between the denser, invisible, dynamic energy—air—we call thinking and our physical brain, further stimulates the electrical currents in our brain which then increase our brains' vitality and capacity to perform. Positive thinking which contains more powerful electrical currents than counteractive thinking is like eating healthful food and exercising. It nourishes our brains, keeps them active and expands their lives.

If indeed there is a close and personal relationship between our thinking and our brains, then what types of experiences should we consider for ourselves? Ones that positively impact and build our lives. Our experiences influence our inner and outer perceptions, which affect our thinking, and our thinking determines the health of our brains. Not only does our thinking impact the vigor of our brains, but all conscious ideas and/or mental images we hold to be true are transferred to our subconscious. The thoughts, ideas and/or mental images, of our subconscious when infused with our emotions and feelings further influence and manifest our experiences in the world of matter. Communication between our physical brains and our mental minds, our conscious and subconscious, is reciprocal and should always be clear, peaceful and constructive in order to have a life filled with peace, beauty, joy and prosperity.

The more we acknowledge God, our Eternal Breath, and make use of its life, intelligence and power the further we increase our mental capacities and come to rely upon them to fulfill our wishes. Our breath is Divine Inspiration, stimulating our conscious minds and beings with harmony and creativity and liberating us from a mundane existence, therefore lifting us into loftier realities. Renewed, we are encouraged to live freely, like water and air, resisting less and trusting more the extraordinariness of life—the magic that perpetually unfolds before us. The individuals who show up in our lives come to assist us, for we attract only relationships that are co-operative and fruitful. The unexpected gifts we receive expand our happiness and demonstrate for us acts of kindness and charity. The unintentional blessings we bestow upon others reflect for us the inexhaustibleness of our good wills and great fortune. The surprises of life are plentiful and peace and joy are for us to experience beyond what we might have imagined. The Universe, as Intelligent Spirit, at all times, conspires with us to bring forth our greatest and highest life, effortlessly and efficiently. When we are awake to this truth we will have come to know what it truly means to experience the way of least resistance—a glorious and abundant life—The Kingdom of God.

*To acknowledge that there is more to us than our physical attributes and basic mental capacities, that there is an intrinsic, invisible energy that exists as part of all that is, is to recognize the life of God.*

An Abundant Life lets us experience the never-ending inspiration, intelligence and benevolence of God. There are many stories I can share which reflect these qualities and that continually remind me of the truth of such an existence, but I will share just one. I have always loved music, primarily the kind that deeply touches my inner being and moves me to dance and sing aloud or to become serene and quiet. Because of my passion for this artistic genre, I've dreamed about meeting artists whose songs I especially enjoy; and I began to write about this modality as a universal language that connects us all, regardless of our exterior differences, customs and creeds. Music allows us to relate to one another without words, and therefore, without barriers real or imagined. In my writing, I further explored music, built a stronger relationship with it and was able to see it as something more than just a means of entertainment. Music is a medium that unites the spiritual, mental, emotional and physical worlds— in more ways than one…

To think and to dream are mental activities. We think in order to interrelate with our experiences, and we dream to bring forth a mental image of an ideal we are interested in materializing. I wrote about music, I talked about how it made me feel and I dreamed about meeting artists who knew how to create magic with rhythm, melody and harmony. Not long after writing my first novel, which included my thoughts on jazz and spiritual song, my world began to concretize my thoughts, feelings and dreams. Although, I had on many occasions attended music concerts that I thoroughly enjoyed, they were rarely free and hadn't afforded me the opportunity to personally meet and thank those who shared their musical skills and talents on stage. Perhaps, I had yet to believe in all of my dreams, but all of my dreams believed in me.

I continued to enjoy and write about music. As well I created opportunities to speak with others regarding its deeper transformative powers. As I did this, I found myself in the company of friends and acquaintances who were either affiliated with musical institutions or who personally knew musical artists, both seasoned and new. I visited New York City quite often. While there I was frequently invited to attend engagements that involved some type of creative and musical activity. I didn't always know who would be at these venues, but I always seemed to meet the most interesting people, including those who were meant to be surprises. One friend I met in New York, invited me to a South African Freedom Day reception. It was a wonderful event. The food was awesome, the live African band was phenomenal, the dancing was inspirational and the conversations were deeply interesting. I was happy that I drove for almost three hours to join in on the fun. As always, I was encouraged by those who I met to stay in touch, so I did. My horizons were being expanded and I was grateful.

In April of 2012, I was in New York to create a commercial for *Wisdom In New Dimensions (WIND)*. While there, I was to attend this year's South African Freedom Day reception. The evening of the event, I dressed for the occasion, caught the subway to Midtown Manhattan and journeyed to the hosting hotel in Time Square. I was ready for good food, great music and dance, inspiring dialogue and new connections. After the introductions and speech which opened the reception, I partook in the meal being served then decided to walk around and mingle. While I scanned the large room I caught the eyes of a South African friend who I met at The Red Rooster restaurant in Harlem only a couple months before. I walked over to him and we talked briefly. He mentioned that in a few days, on April 30, 2012, the first annual *International Jazz Day* concert would take place there in the City. Of course, I was interested. I asked, "How can I get a ticket?"

On the day of the first annual *International Jazz Day* Sunset Concert in New York—the Sunrise Concert took place in New Orleans during the morning—I visited the building where my South African friend worked. After arriving and intro-ducing myself to the receptionist another South African friend, who I met as well at the restaurant, walked out with a sheet of paper in his hand. It included the time of the concert, the location and the names of the hosting organizations, which were the *Thelonious Monk Institute of Jazz* and *UNESCO,* the *United Nations Educational, Scientific and Cultural Organization*; but he did not have a ticket for me. And I would not know if one would be available until I showed up at the location. When I got there, I waited at the gate for my friend to arrive, then found out he still hadn't acquired an extra ticket for me. Yet I knew I was suppose to attend this concert. My intuition told me so, therefore, I prayed that a ticket would appear. The

Sunset Concert would begin at 7:00 p.m. It was now almost starting time but still no ticket. The security crew and VIP host at the gate where I stood talked to me and encouraged my faith. They too believed that someone would come with an extra ticket. My waiting was not in vain. Not only did a guest show up at approximately 6:55 p.m. with an extra ticket, but I had the opportunity to greet and speak to VIP guests who many of us know and who would ensure that I also received an invitation to the post concert reception. At the post concert reception, I was in the company of, and in conversation with, many amazing artists, including the remarkable musician and singer Stevie Wonder, Goodwill Ambassador, Herbie Hancock, the extraordinary percussionist, Sheila E and the exceptional, young bassist, Esperanza Spalding. Let me not forget to mention that Quincy Jones, Chaka Khan and Tony Bennett among other gifted vocalists shared their voices, and musical geniuses their instrumental sounds with us live during the concert. My dream came true. It was no longer just a thought, written words on screen and in a book or colorful visual ideas. My dream was now tangible. All I had to do was completely open myself to the full life meant for me, follow my intuition and let inspiration lead me forward. Abundance is truly—good music. Good music is like the harmony of heaven—The Kingdom of God within us all.

*To live a life of abundance
it is necessary for us to have
keen perceptibilities, and
to know that improvisation
is largely for the purpose
of allowing us to
surprise ourselves.*

-   *Dana Rondel*

# Chapter 9
## Sharing With Others

*You are to become a creator, not a competitor; you are going to get what you want, but in such a way that when you get it every other man will have more than he has now.*

- Wallace D. Wattles

Service implies an ability to give. It suggests that we have something of value that others can benefit from. Service can be provided in myriad ways, but the best way is by doing what we truly love. To give of ourselves by means of thoughtful, selfless and genuine acts is to experience the highest form of charity. When we give in this way we not only heighten someone else's life, but we allow for a harmonious flow of goodwill and fortune. Giving, part of the organic, reciprocal fluidity of the Universe, is energy containing electrical transmitters which communicate the vibrational tone of an act. What is meant is, that when we give from a space of authentic kindness, the receiver of our service, whatever it might be, will as well experience feelings that are associated with kindness, such as gratitude. Our service, being the impetus for the expression of gratitude experienced by the receiver, will in turn allow us to as well experience gratitude. The relationship between giver and receiver is a mutual one, so that each person involved benefit tremendously. Service then is an act that increases the well-being of others as well as our own when we are giving from our divine hearts, the fountain of unconditional love.

Giving is altruistic. Altruism as defined by the dictionary is, *the principle or practice of loving concern for or devotion to the welfare of others.* As children, we were taught the importance of sharing. What we shared and how we shared reflected the quality of our relationship with ourselves and with others. If, at an early age, we were informed that we would always have what we need and desire, we would give knowing our supply is endless, and therefore, we would give without concern. If on the other hand, we heard words that expressed, "not enough" this generally causes us to completely hold back or limit our giving. The Universe being reciprocal, expresses life by means of harmony and equilibrium. Its flow is constant and it always has what it needs. If we expressed the same reciprocity in our lives we too would have more than enough rather than not enough. To experience reciprocity we must be willing to give as well as receive. Altruism lets us experience the act of giving as an act of generosity. To be generous signifies: I am willing and able to provide you with something of mine that will be of value to you. In doing so, I will not have depleted my supply. I will still have everything I currently require to live peacefully. When we practice altruism we create a perception in our subconscious minds that our wellsprings of riches will never run out; therefore, we will always be able to give, and we will always receive to keep our wellsprings of riches continually flowing. The perception we create in the material world is, that we are wealthy beyond measure, and therefore, we give to also create wealth for others. To ensure the validity of this truth, we will continually be open to receive the gifts that too add to our lives.

Compensation is to receive a fair exchange for what is being provided. Give what you want to receive in return. Comply with the golden principle: *Do unto others as you want others to do unto you,* within every transaction in life and you will gain what you have earned. The transactions that I am speaking about do not just consist of those concerning services, goods and currency, but with all interchanges and exchanges. When someone says to me, "I wish I had good friends who I could depend on," my response is, "Simply be a good and reliable friend." If you seek honesty within your relationships, be honest with all persons. If you seek unconditional love, give unconditional love unfailingly. If you seek empathy, be understanding of other people and their experiences. If you seek trust, be trusting. Whatever you seek to have in life give it and in the process of doing so, you will create a channel which allows for its return. And yet, although a channel is created upon giving, receptivity, our willingness to receive, is necessary to draw what is to come to us.

What we give and what we receive have value: service, goods, money, friendship, honesty, unconditional love, empathy and trust, etc. However, the worth that we associate with our service, our goods, our property, such as cash, our relationships and each of the aforementioned qualities, is relative. Each individual determines for him/herself the importance of his/her service and goods, of the relationships and the interchanges within them, and the significance of money and what can be garnered by it. How we come to decide on the level of importance or significance of anyone or anything depends on our learning and/or our perceptions of ourselves, others and of life itself. Mutuality, the quality of mutual respect, nonetheless, causes us to consider further the value of what we give and what we receive. If we believe others are worthy of more we give more. If we believe we are worthy of more we allow ourselves more. And at no time are we or others careful or unwilling to receive the more that is being given, simply because of the respect and worth we have defined for our lives. Compensation is therefore, the interchange of respect and appreciation and the exchange of services and goods that add value to our lives and the lives of others and heightens each of our senses of self-worth, our perceptions and our experiences.

*Who's the judge?*
The Judge is God!
*Why is [God] God?*
Because God decides who
wins or loses, not my opponent!
*Who's your opponent?*
He doesn't exist!
*Why does he not exist?*
Because he is merely a
dissenting voice to the truth
I speak!

- The Great Debaters, Film

Strategy. What is it? It is a concept or concepts employed to bring about a desired result. What does it mean to strategize? To strategize is to confide in our ability to creatively think of ways to build on current ideas. In the process of creative thinking our imaginations are utilized to bring forth pictures of a completed scenario. As we see a desired and completed scenario within our minds we are then driven to materialize our vision into concrete form. Generally, this entails collecting data which allows us to know who, what, when, where and how we will meet our aims. Once we have this information we are then apt to take the necessary steps to attain our goals. Strategy then allows for a clear, simple, effective and purposeful approach to fulfill our objectives. Our intentions are made plain and our attention and concentration is focused on only what is required to accomplish a request or an end, whether our own or someone else's.

How does strategy differ from competition? Competition is to go after someone or something you believe belongs to you. In most cases we are moved to compete. To compete requires us to take on the person(s) and/or thing(s) we perceive to be in the way of who or what we want. As we know, sports generally require individuals to challenge one another's endurance and skills necessary to win games or contests. In education, exams are given to test teachers' techniques and students' aptitudes and learning; in business, companies vie for specific markets by employing advertisements meant to appeal to the greatest number of consumers' imaginations. Religion, seeks to attract the masses by professing to know the truth of God. Competition in sports, academia, business and religion all vary, but with each a challenge is presented that must be overcome to attain a desired end. In sports, teams work to overcome losing. In academia, students work to overcome failing. In business, companies work to overcome losses. In religion, leaders and their congregations work to overcome transgressions. Is it necessary to focus on overcoming losing, failing, loss and/or transgressions if we no longer perceive that a challenge or wrong exists? If all we see is opportunity, then how would this change the game in sports, learning and business? If all we see is growth then how would this transform the dynamics of religion? In sports, strategy nullifies competition when each team focuses on co-operation within its team. Cooperation unifies, strengthens and builds teams, allowing for greater endurance and skill rather than allowing for the depletion of energy due to the idea that an object(s) is in the way. Strategy says, there is only one object to focus on—the place where the point is made. Competition says, there are two or more objects to focus on, therefore, diverting attention and weakening concentration. The opportunity is for co-operation. Co-operation dismisses the idea that a challenge exists and therefore the focus is solely on opportunity. In academia, strategy invalidates competition when teachers motivate forward movement by encouraging students to exclusively focus on enhancing their thinking and insight. Clear thinking allows for the revealing of higher truths, and insight allows for greater visions and perceptions of life which make room for the creation of new paradigms. Strategy says, failure does not exist, therefore, attention and concentration remain on openness, creativity and achievement. Competition says, there is always a race between inadequacy and progress, and therefore, attention and concentration are divided between failing and succeeding. In business, strategy negates competition when companies primarily focus on inspiration to garner new and brilliant ideas. Inspiration utilizes intelligence and power to bring forth artistic solutions that uplift and encourage movement toward an ideal, rather than pull or push individuals toward an ideal. Strategy says, there is more than enough of everything for everyone and therefore attention and concentration always remain on imaginative solutions and gain. Competition says, there is not enough and therefore attention and concentration remain on survival. In religion, strategy absolves competition when organizations and communities focus on reverence for God alone.

Reverence for God allows us to acknowledge the Omnipresence, Omniscience and Omnipotence of our Creator which gives breath, intelligence and power to us equally. Strategy says, let us individually and together seek the highest truth already inside us each and learn and make use of this truth for harmony, greater love and prosperity. Competition says, God's intelligence and power are limited to only a few, and therefore only the chosen will experience the Kingdom of God. The rest will be denied.

Energy is transmitted with every thought, with every feeling and with every act. Strategy unites, creates and builds. Competition divides, breaks down and weakens. Both strategy and competition require thought, feeling and action which put out energy that draws to them like energy; therefore, what we know or believe to be true for our lives or the lives of others, sets the foundation for all other truths that will determine our experiences. If our attention and concentration are focused on unity, love and good fortune so will we experience cooperation, healthy relations and growth. If our attention and concentration are focused on fear, denial and limitation so will we experience similar energies. And yet the opportunity to know and see differently is always before us letting us at all times modify our perceptions and positively transform every experience. Strategy reminds us that we are creators with unlimited resources within and around us, and so we at no time need to give competition a purpose to exist.

*What we create for ourselves we too create for others, which means we add not only to our own lives but to the lives of others.*

*Increasing our supply is to give more and to receive more. Always expect greater and the Universe will co-operate to make it so.*

What experiences do you want to share with others? What do you want to see when you look out your windows or walk out your door? See the truth. We can never experience lack or limitation, simply because we will always have everything we absolutely need directly inside of ourselves. We have the capacity to think, to envision, to communicate and to create exactly what we want for our world, so our world should always reflect peace, love, happiness and prosperity, our living and unwavering faith in good. Our individual exper- iences are those that we will inevitably share with others; and because life is reciprocal the return on our investments of thoughtfulness, selflessness and authenticity will be gifts that will greatly benefit and add value to all of our lives. We truly are rich beyond measure. This truth we should consciously live as we are creating for ourselves and sharing with others.

*Seek nothing outside of yourself*
*for inspiration, wisdom and power,*
*and yet let all life inspire you,*
*by witnessing at all times its magic*
*which invariably unfolds before us,*
*moving us in its rhythm —*
*a melodic and dazzling song…*

- Dana Rondel

# Chapter 10
# Doing More That Matters

*Don't Worry, Be Happy*

- Bobby McFerrin

Don't worry, be happy... In April 2007, I was able to see Bobby McFerrin sing live at an Omega spiritual conference I attended in New York City. The conference attendees included a community of well known spiritual leaders, teachers and writers, holistic health practitioners, vendors and those who were seeking to know more about themselves and the world we live in. The speakers were dynamic, the seminars were informative and the entertainment was extremely uplifting. I especially remember Bobby McFerrin's performance. It was awe-inspiring. The music he made with his mouth and body, instruments used by God, deeply moved me. After the conference, I sought to learn more about this phenomenal man and of course I went out and acquired his music. Bobby McFerrin is an individual who urged me to discover more about the breath of life, which made for the magic we witnessed and felt when he released song from himself. There were no external objects needed, just the inspiration contained within. To share the gift of song that's organic and beautiful, requires one to not only know God but to know himself.

I learned what truly makes for the poetry of life—the way we use our breath. Poetry, plainly, is a musical composition of our experiences expressed through elevated thoughts and imaginative images, written, spoken or sung. The dynamic, vibrational currents within the rhythm and melody of sound and words have the power to change our internal frequencies and the external energies that surround us. Poetry, like dance, is magic, given life by breath and movement. When you consider this thought, what comes forth in your mind? And what do you begin to feel? I think life, and I feel good. The air and water in and of our existence determines our outlook, our experiences and our creations. When Bobby McFerrin sung to us live in April of 2007, his song, "Don't worry, be happy," simply meant, our thoughts (air) and feelings (water) make for the life we'll live. Therefore, don't worry, just be happy. God is always on our side, and as long as we too are on our sides, so will life be.

The more I began to learn about the organic power imbued within our thoughts, words, feelings and actions, the more I realized the truth of our existence. We have a choice about what we want to give power to and how we want to live. We can choose what we think, what we say, how we feel and what we do in any given moment. So why wouldn't we want to live the very best life we can? The power is with us, therefore:

*We will think the greatest and highest thoughts and give life to our ideas…*

*We will speak the greatest and highest words and give song and color to our visions…*

*We will feel the greatest and highest dynamic, vibrational currents of our hearts and shape our dreams…*

*We will learn to free ourselves of thinking and let go of our thoughts – this is how we tune-in to the secrets of God.*

*We will practice observing life in the midst of a silent and still mind – this is how we come to know Life.*

*We will relate to our experiences without analyzing and defining them – this is how magic is made.*

*And we will invariably allow for the surprises of God...*

Poetry is magic, breath and movement, giving life to the song God is singing for us. To know and hear this song we must first realize that Life is already full, complete and perfect within itself, requiring nothing else except for our exuberant participation. Let us therefore live and be free together in a world that wants us to add to its beauty by co-operating and co-creating with it. Let us share our joy and let our growth be the wisdom unfailingly teaching others—*doing more that matters* requires only our willingness to reverence and acknowledge God, and to love ourselves, others and life.

- What is your very best life?

- Do you have a strategy (your blueprint) that will allow you to bring this life to fruition?

- Begin your journey now...

   (1)   Think the idea—This is Idealization.

   (2)   See the complete vision—This is Visualization.

(3)    Keep your attention and concentration on the vision as you take the
steps to bring your dream to full life
—This is Materialization.


Remember, God is always co-operating and co-creating with us, therefore, conspiring to bring forth our greatest and highest good. And as well, there's magic in all of life, continually unfolding before us sundry surprises to make us smile. Enjoy the journey…

*Look To This Day*

*For it is Life, the very Life of Life.*
*In its brief course lie all the Verities and*
*Realities of your existence;*
*The Bliss of Growth;*
*The Glory of Action;*
*The Splendor of Beauty;*
*For Yesterday is but a Dream,*
*And To-morrow is only a Vision;*
*But To-Day well lived makes every*
*Yesterday a Dream of Happiness, and*
*Every To-morrow a Vision of Hope.*
*Look well, therefore, to This Day.*

-    Sanscrit

# Chapter 11
# Putting It All Into Perspective

*My Priority is Perfection...*

*Albeit my thoughts are invisible, they lift me, and although my thinking is not seen, it is clear. My mental mind reflects perfect health.*

*Albeit my emotions are without form, I feel inspiration. My emotional body reflects perfect health.*

*Albeit my body is material, it is divine. My physical body reflects perfect health.*

.

*I am the almighty vessel of God. I am truth. I am real.*

Writing this book is a wonderful and enlightening journey. I experience so much joy in the process of recalling and revealing wisdom that has and still does inspire, transform and uplift my life. As mentioned in my introduction, all truths within the pages of this text are those that I live. They bring me to a place inside myself that at one time I had not fathomed, and they open doors for me to greater truths and higher realities. The peace, pleasure and potential I experience because of what I now know is beyond what words can express, but I have tried to with affirmations that I included on preceding and forthcoming pages. I pray they will benefit you tremendously and you too will live the life created by *Good Will, Good Works* and *Good Fortune*.

To say *Life is Good* is to declare the grandness of God, and to convey the depth, beauty and power of divine love; so I think and speak the words, *Life is Good*, as often as possible, yet most times unconsciously. They are inherently a part of my life. I know this because, at times I come upon signs that share this exact phrase: *Life is Good;* or sometimes I see these words on bumper stickers, T-shirts and written or engraved on some other object or paraphernalia. Clearly, my subconscious mind lives with this knowing, and therefore, my life cont-inually reflects the greatest and highest good.

On the pages that follow, my intent is to put all that I communicated in earlier chapters into perspective. I want you to remember the principles that are important and to apply them daily. As you read them, mentally and verbally affirm the truths that speak loudest to you. Let them move your life toward the goals, visions and dreams you have made for yourself. Hear them when you are busy at other things but want to stay connected to the inspiration within you. No matter what you are doing always be inspired. Your bright outlook will be the foremost vision that colors all other thoughts, visions and dreams, so see the truth of God—there is only *Good* in you, in others and in the world.

Affirmation: *My prayers are simply to convey my gratitude for all that is already done. I thank you, God, for allowing me to know beyond my physical sight.*

*I believe that you're great, that there's something magnificent about you. Regardless of what has happened to you in your life, regardless of how young or how old you think you might be, the moment you begin to think properly, this something that is within you, this power within you that's greater than the world, it will begin to emerge. It will take over your life. It will feed you, it will clothe you, it will guide you, protect you, direct you, sustain your very existence. If you let it! Now that is what I know, for sure.* - Dr. Michael Bernard Beckwith

*"God works unceasingly, and so do I," - John 5:17. There is never a time when we are apart from God, who is at all times in everyone, in everything and in every place. Therefore, let us acknowledge God regardless of what we're doing, for it is God who gives us all that we will ever need, allowing for our lives to constantly be full, complete and perfect.* – Dana Rondel

*Every day will be full to overflowing with blessings of every conceivable state or being. Every succeeding day will become richer and larger than the days that have gone before, as we become more and more conscious of the great truth, that God is giving us everything today that is needed to make this the greatest day we ever knew. And in all our efforts we will be guided, to the end that we may invariably do what is best, knowing that a higher power will be with us so long as we live and work for the larger life and the greatest good.*
– Christian D. Larson

*Learn to keep the door shut, keep out of your mind and out of your world every element that seeks admittance with no definite helpful end in view.* – George Matthew Adams

*This above all: To thine ownself be true, and it must follow, as the night the day, thou canst not then be false to any man.* – Shakespeare

*"… when man awakens to the truth, and affirms his oneness with all Life, he finds that he takes on the clear eye, the elastic step, the vigour of youth; he finds that he has discovered the source of all power.* – Charles F. Haanel

*What you get by achieving your goals is not as important as what you become by achieving your goals.* - Goethe

*In the daytime of our lives, we have the sun. In the night, we have the moon. There is never a time when we are without a higher guiding light.* – Dana Rondel

Affirmation: *The Universe (God) always conspires to bring about, into manifestation, the greatest and highest good for my life, according to the deepest truths of my mind and heart.*

*But God commands: And do not be conformed to this world, but be transformed by the renewing of your mind.* – Romans 12:2

*The conscious mind uses words to categorize and define our experiences. The subconscious mind uses images and symbols, which give us various perceptions. Our thinking, thoughts and mental images assist in creating our realities.* – Dana Rondel

*I dream my painting and I paint my dream.*
– Vincent van Gogh

*Aerodynamically, the bumblebee shouldn't be able to fly, but the bumble bee doesn't know it, so it goes on flying anyway.* – Mary Kay Ash

*If you want to awaken all of humanity, then awaken all of yourself, if you want to eliminate the suffering in the world, then eliminate all that is [destructive] and negative in yourself. Truly, the greatest gift you have to give is that of your own self-transformation.* – Lao Tzu

*You yourself, as much as anybody in the entire universe, deserve your love and affection.*
– Siddhartha Gautama

Affirmation: *I free from within me all that I have no intention on prospering. I internalize only that which I plan to build and make stronger.*

Affirmation: *My thinking, thoughts and visions determine the height of my realities, therefore, I choose to think only those thoughts that lift me to the highest heights of my life.*

*Every person we encounter and every reality that unfolds in our lives has a gift for us, to know what it is we must always be fully present within the experience.* – Dana Rondel

*Success is knowing that one other human being [breathes] a little easier because you [live].*
– Dr. Dennis Kimbro

*The best and most beautiful things in the world cannot be seen or even touched – they must be felt with the heart.* – Helen Keller

Affirmation: *I relate to rather than react to this experience to receive from it only the greatest good that is intended for me.*

*Our conscious and subconscious make up our mental minds, the thinking and thoughts we cannot see, but are present. Our mental minds relay information to our physical brains regarding our internal truths and world. Our physical brains, associated with our physical senses, relay information to our mental minds regarding the external world. The relationship between our mental minds, conscious and subconscious, and our physical brains is reciprocal. What we hold to be true in our internal and external worlds, in our mental minds and physical brains, are then given form by our constructive, emotional feelings. Our thoughts, which most influence our perceptions and create our realities can be cleared from our subconscious and be replaced with new thoughts at anytime. Generally, we are most in touch with our subconscious during meditation and rest. And it is during this time when the conscious mind is silent and still that we receive our greatest inspiration and truths. Our mental minds and physical brains are given life by the same breath that imbues all life, including our*

*thinking and thoughts. It is also important to know that our constructive thoughts and feelings always vanish destructive thoughts and feelings. Our positive thoughts and feelings vibrate higher and are much more powerful.*
– Dana Rondel

Affirmation: *I embody the qualities and characteristics of the One, Changeless and Harmonious God.*

*The secret of power is the recognition of the Omnipresent, Omniscient and Omnipotent Life.* – Dana Rondel

*The longer we are able to hold positive thoughts in our minds, the more powerful the positive energy around us becomes. We don't need to focus on action and controlling so much when we are surrounded by energy that draws what we want toward us. We can simply respond to the opportunities that naturally come our way. When this is the essence of our experience, we can go with the flow, knowing that we will be okay.* – Anonymous

Affirmation: *I put everything in the hands of God. I rely on only God for all things and have faith and trust that God will draw to me those of the highest order to bring forth the manifestations I have wished for. My living faith and trust in God always prevails.*

Affirmation: *Opportunities are endless, possibilities are infinite and we are wise and powerful.*

*We are not here to be living bodies of theory, we are here to be living truths, expressing for ourselves, others and the world God's miraculous creation as Spiritual-Human Beings.* – Dana Rondel

*To acknowledge that there is more to us than our physical attributes, that there is an ever-present, invisible energy that exists as part of all that is, is to recognize the life of God.*
– Dana Rondel

*It is clear…that thoughts of abundance will respond only to similar thoughts; the wealth of the individual is seen to be what he inherently is. Affluence within is found to be the secret of attraction for affluence without. The ability to produce is found to be the real source of wealth of the individual. It is for this reason that he who has his heart in his work is certain to meet with unbounded success. He will give and continually give, and the more he gives the more he will receive.* – Charles F. Haanel

*Follow the path of least resistance, for it leads to the world of abundance.* – Dana Rondel

*To accomplish anything in life we must co-operate and co-create with the infinite, unchanging law – God. If we do so we shall always be successful.* – Dana Rondel

*People become really quite remarkable when they start thinking that they can do things. When they believe in themselves they have the first secret of success.* – Norman Vincent Peale

*When we love, we always strive to become better than we are. When we strive to become better than we are, everything around us becomes better too.* – Paulo Coelho

*If you treat an individual as he is, he will remain how he is. But if you treat him as if he were what he ought to be and could be, he will become what he ought to be and could be.* – Goethe

*The law of success is service — the act of thoughtful giving and allowance of its benefits.* – Dana Rondel

*The law of growth — prosperity — is dependent on faith and reciprocity. We must never doubt our abilities and we must give to receive and to receive more we must give more.* – Dana Rondel

*The vibration of harmony (silence) found in life and music is the interconnecting element of all existence — it is the universal language in which we each relate one to another without dependence on any other internal or external energy.* – Dana Rondel

*While I know myself as a creation of God, I am also obligated to realize and remember that everyone else and everything else are also God's creation.* – Maya Angelou

*To truly live life is to experience it to its fullest. To do so is to relate to our experiences without analyzing and defining them. It is our thinking that causes us to break apart and compartmentalize our experiences. To simply observe life in the midst of a silent and still*

*mind is to know life beyond itself, to know it as full, perfect and complete within itself rather than as separate parts creating a whole.*
– Dana Rondel

*Omnipresence is pure breath - pure breath is divine inspiration. Omniscience is absolute silence - absolute silence is infinite intelligence. Omnipotence is absolute stillness - absolute stillness is eternal power.* – Dana Rondel

*Spirituality – the merging of religion and science; it is our air and our water.*
– Dana Rondel

*We are the image and likeness of God – God's Spirit and our spirit are the same.*
– Dana Rondel

*The Full-Life is our Divinity and Freedom.*
– Dana Rondel

*Gratitude increases our happiness and blessings.* – Dana Rondel

Affirmation: *God's Way is clear and simple…*

Affirmation: *Life is Good…*

*The journey of self-discovery is enriched by our connection to God. The realization that each individual is a part of God, serves to enhance our spiritual growth and our capacity to perform acts of kindness. The strength of our unity lies in the recognition of God in each and every human being. When we assemble as one, we express the deepest unity of God.*

*All are invited here, at every level. Our differences shall emerge as strengths, as we give to one another, as we flourish, and as we grow. Our unity is an extension of our connection to God and our connection to one another.*

*- Judaic Wisdom*

# Omniversal Life International (OLI)
## Life and Leadership Models & Strategies

## Part I.
## Models and Strategies: The Blue Print

## Model: Effectual Communication

Everything has breath. It is an ubiquitous, life-giving energy. In its purest essence it is inert, silent and still, allowing there to be no end to its vitality within us and in our external world. To consciously use this energy for our sundry benefits we must be aware of it and make use of it. Breath determines our inner and outer strength, our endurance, the height of our attitudes and optimism, our fluidity with others and with life and the clarity and effectiveness of our communication, among many other things. So it is important that the flow of breath circulating throughout our bodies is uninhibited by lower vibrational thoughts and emotions that are not conducive to our overall well-being.

## Strategy: Breathing and Clear Expression

Breathing is an unconscious effort stimulated by our subconscious minds and physical brains; nonetheless to ensure the daily vigor and internal harmony of our breathing, it is of great value to become conscious of our breath during periods of rest, and to feel our breath moving freely throughout every part of our bodies. It is also a great idea to further arouse our breath by intermittently increasing and decreasing our breathing primarily through our nose. Doing so, will boost our energy, allow for clearer thinking, raise our thoughts and influence more fluent articulation. Renewing of internal energy also takes place through rapid fire breaths, inhaling quickly through our noses then blowing out quickly through our mouths. As you perform your breathing techniques, focus on the area of your body where you intend to renew your energy.

*The greatest discovery of all time is that a person can change his future by merely changing his attitude [altitude].*

– Oprah Winfrey

## Model: Solution Acquisitioning

A problem cannot exist when a solution does. As a matter of truth, problems have no life unless we give them life. I always choose to give only creative solutions life, for they allow for healthier thinking and more desirable results and experiences. Whether or not the exact solution I need is always in the forefront of my mind is of no relevance, the idea is to simply have a solution. When you focus on a solution, whatever it might be, you are giving life to the notion that the goal is already attained. Also, having one solution generally expands to more solutions and/or the ideal solution. As you consider the solution(s) answer: who, what, when, where and how. Doing so will further increase the energy necessary to meet your aim.

## Strategy: Intuitive Silence

The first and necessary step to garner a great solution for your endeavor(s) is to receive the answers to these questions:

- What is the purpose for this endeavor and/or experience?

- What do I (we) want?

After the questions are asked, whether quietly or aloud, become silent and still. It doesn't matter where you are, simply give yourself several moments or more for silence. As you are doing this expect the most ideal answers to come. When they do embrace them, begin to expand on them and keep moving forward.

## Strategy: Active Listening

To hear the intuitive voice within active listening is required. Active listening is the radar of hearing which allows us to directly engage the deeper wisdom that is revealing itself to us within silence. This deeper wisdom then gives us clear and simple instructions we are to follow to reach a desired end.

## Model: Thought Awareness

To be consciously aware of our thoughts at all times requires discipline and effort. It is important to keep out of our minds all thinking and thoughts that do not add value to our lives and that could interfere with our achieving our definite plans.

## Strategy: Sound Thinking

Clear thinking is our ability to focus on only what we are intending to create; and it necessitates constructive perceptions that keep our attention on the highest reality. What we think and hold on to is what we will concretize in our natural world.

To practice clear thinking begin to simplify your life. Ask yourself:

- What really matters to me?

- What requires my full participation in order to fulfill my aspirations?

As you think about these questions, embrace optimism. Optimism will allow you to see more clearly the purpose of each aspiration as well as to know how it will add more meaning to your life. When your life is more simple you become less distracted by what doesn't matter, and you become consciously aware of only what does. We must direct our thinking rather than let our thinking direct us.

## Model: Mental Discipline and Focus

The mind is like a still body of water, quiet and calm. Our thinking is the air moving within it and determining the condition of its internal atmosphere, whether our thoughts will be clouded or clear. It is always a good practice to silence and still the mind, which is when it is functioning at its highest and bringing us more desirable outcomes.

Mirroring is the mind's ability to reflect on the outside what is on the inside. External quiet and calm will mirror our internal quiet and calm. Our outer experiences and realities are great indicators of the thinking and thoughts from within.

## Strategy: Stillness Meditation

Find a comfortable area to sit or rest. Once you have, be still and begin to silence your mind by allowing the current energy, your thinking and thoughts, to be released. If your thinking continues do not engage it, consciously turn it off. If previous thoughts, particularly those within the subconscious mind, begin to surface do not engage them either, simply allow them to release themselves. As you continue this practice eventually your thinking will end, all thoughts will dissipate and your mind will become clear. Remember, it has taken a great level of discipline for many to finally reach the point of silence and stillness, yet it is achievable if you are persistent. Simply continue to focus your attention on nothing at all.

## Strategy: Attention and Concentration

A silent and still mind is a mind at its greatest potential. It is during this innate phase of mind that your thinking, thoughts, perceptions and reflections are most clear. It allows for your focus to be concentrated on only what you are aspiring to create. To begin your practice of concentration, begin to pay attention to an idea that is part of a greater vision you are endeavoring to fulfill. As you focus your mind on this idea see it growing in your mind.

- What is the idea?

- How does it look?

Continue to see it expanding into your inner vision—the mental image of the idea. Let nothing else enter into your mind to distract your attention from the objective you are now concentrating on. Give the idea and vision more power by continuing to focus on it until it is clear, full, complete and perfect in your mind. When you are satisfied that the idea has been fulfilled then you have achieved it. It is only a matter of time for your idea to become your reality. Let the idea be a great one.

## Model: Creative Conceptualization

Creative Conceptualization is to experience an ideal or dream in your mind before it becomes real in the physical world. It goes beyond simply focusing your attention and concentration on an idea and/or vision. You can now see the full, complete and perfect manifestation in your mind.

## Strategy: Inspired Visioning

- What does your new reality look like?

- What do you hear while engaged in the experience?

- How does the experience make you feel?

- What smells are prevalent, etc.?

You are fully present within an experience in your mental mind, and therefore, giving it more color and density so that it will come into being in the real world as you have envisioned. Expect that there might be surprises and they will always be those that will bring further joy.


# Model: Truth Endorsement

We all adopt truths that become the foundation for our lives. These truths will give birth to other truths which will most likely become our individual experiences. When we choose to embrace a truth as our own we are choosing to endorse it, to give it more life.

## Strategy: Affirmative Writing

As an inspirational writer it is easy for me to write affirmative truths that I know will continually inspire me as well as others. I also know that writing my thoughts on screen or on paper gives them added life and increases their existence. Written words are no longer just thoughts we can release from our minds once we have no use for them. They become the stepping stones we lay to lead us toward another experience.

- Where do you want your words to lead you?

- What will that experience entail?

*We know that the Universal Thought has for its goal the creation of form, and we know that the individual thought is likewise forever attempting to express itself in form, and we know that the word is a thought form, and a sentence is a combination of thought forms, therefore, if we wish our ideal to be beautiful or strong, we must see that the words out of which this temple will eventually be created are exact, that they are put together carefully, because accuracy in building words and sentences is the highest form of architecture in civilization and is a passport to success.* – Charles F. Haanel

Think clearly and affirmatively and you will write beautiful, uplifting and influential words that will make for you glorious experiences which will be your magnificent reality.

## Part II.
## Models and Strategies: The Full Creation

### Model: Mastering Mind

I am the Master over my mind. My thinking is inspired by internal and external perceptions that create for my life the greatest and highest realities. I can at any time choose what thoughts will take hold within. At no time will I allow thinking or thoughts that will draw away from me peace, joy and prosperity, the inherent treasures of my living and unwavering faith and existence.

*There is no Power but God in life, in our lives and in the world. God is All there is.*

## Strategy: Co-operation and Co-creation

I at all times fully co-operate and co-create with God, the Omnipresent, Omniscient and Omnipotent Life; the pure and harmonious breath of my existence.

## Model: Power Praying

My thinking, thoughts and words have life, intelligence and power. I will think clearly, I will embrace optimism and I will speak constructively. I recognize that God knows my mind and my heart for we are one, and therefore, I will expect nothing but I will allow for everything I have aspired for. Abundance is our Universe and too is within me, so I endlessly draw to me the sundry treasures of Life. And I allow gratitude to be my daily prayer.

## Strategy: Acknowledging

I acknowledge that I am fully alive. I too acknowledge that God is the life that gives me life; the intelligence that gives me wisdom, and the power that illuminates my entire being. I am because God is.

## Model: Freeing Mind

I will observe life without analyzing or defining it. Life is full, complete and perfect and therefore there is nothing I need to add to it. So within each today, I will participate in the life that already is, yet I am here to live, and to live is to dream those dreams that create the greatest and highest reality for my life.

## Strategy: Live Freely, Freely Live

True freedom is granted when we come to know who and what we truly are, which can only be known by first seeing with our inner eye.

- Close your physical eyes.

- Silence your thoughts.

- Still your mind.

- Insight speaks. Listen.

- Observe its truth.

- Open your eyes and know beyond knowing what is real.

- Give thanks. Life is our greatest and highest gift.

- Choice is an infinite opportunity.

- We as full-beings, freed from ourselves, are our most glorious potential.

Inspiration and Imagination are always at work, influencing our ideas, visions and dreams—those that can only be conceived with God. Inspiration feeds life and life feeds imagination—opening our minds to splendid possibilities, ones we have the power to actualize. And yet when we allow our minds to be silent and still we may come to know that the greatest dream is not one desired, but the dream that comes into existence as we allow ourselves to simply be, therefore revealing to us what is deepest within us. For life is a joyful dance encouraging us to improvise with its harmony, melody and rhythm, in order that we might experience its true magic, the surprises and promises of God we least expect, because they are more than we pictured for ourselves. Let us be because our breath is real. Let us be, because great love is what we feel. Let us be, because our lives we need not define. Let us be, because everything we need is inside. Let us be, because gratitude alone makes our world go round. Let us be, because God's truth is beautiful and profound. Let us be, because we have the choice to live. Let us be, because there's so much of life to receive and to give. Let us simply be…

*God is Grand… Love is Divine… Life is Good…*

*The secret of a good life is to live quietly to receive the highest wisdom and to live calmly to receive the greatest power.*

*It is our choice to let inspiration
open our minds, and to let our minds
open our imaginations.*

- *Dana Rondel*

# Notes

# Notes

# Omniversal Life International (OLI)
## Life and Leadership Program

*Think truly, and thy thoughts*
*Shall the world's famine feed;*
*Speak truly, and each word of thine*
*Shall be a fruitful seed;*
*Live truly, and thy life shall be*
*A great and noble creed.*

### - Horatio Bonar

*Omniversal Life International (OLI)* provides the necessary training, tools and wisdom to become a wiser and happier individual as well as a renowned leader in the professional world. Our leaders, those who have been trained within the OLI Life & Leadership Program, have the capacity to guide others toward outcomes that allow for healthier relationships, greater personal and professional growth and higher tangible returns. What makes *Omniversal Life International (OLI)* different? Our Life & Leadership Program is based on spiritual principles that are universal and effective.

Like *Wisdom In New Dimensions (WIND)*, we want you and/or your organization to greatly benefit from the invaluable insight gained through the OLI Life & Leadership Program, therefore we would like you to visit our web site and learn more about us:

www.windinc.org

*A Brighter Life Awaits Us All…*

\-   *Dana Rondel*

# Wisdom In New Dimensions (WIND)

*One With God, In Harmony With All...*

www.windinc.org

*In the beginning, when God created the universe, the earth was formless and desolate. The ocean that covered everything was engulfed in total darkness, and the Spirit of God (Wind) was moving over the water. Then God commanded,*

*"Let there be light" – and light appeared.*
-    *Genesis 1:1-3*

*Wisdom In New Dimensions (WIND) Foundation, Temple & Spiritual Center* formed for the purpose of building and empowering lives by creating stronger ecumenical communities. We are global, and therefore, we seek to reach you wherever you are.

The overall endeavor of the *WIND Foundation, Temple & Spiritual Center* is to raise consciousness and elevate souls through the creative and universal arts and sciences. By raising consciousness and increasing self-knowledge one becomes more aware of the expansiveness of the mental mind and intuitive insight of the heart, which allows for a more fruitful, love-centered and peaceful life.

*Wisdom In New Dimensions (WIND)* is panoptic (all-embracing), or what we call Omniversal (all-inclusive). We accept all faiths, tribes, genders, cultures and ethnicities as part of our family. Our heart's creed is simply: higher truth, love, joy, kindness, oneness, prosperity, generosity, affirmative speech, conscious creation, balanced and healthy living and peace. These are the spiritual principles which we practice daily in all relationships and environments, familiar and unfamiliar.

We would love to have you as part of our spiritual community. Join us as we continue to inform, inspire and uplift the world...

*Things do not change, WE change.*

- Henry David Thoreau

# Notes

# Notes